THE REFORMERS OF EGYPT

The Muslim Institute

Science, Technology and Development in the
Muslim World

Ziauddin Sardar

The Reformers of Egypt

M.A. ZAKI BADAWI

CROOM HELM LONDON

© 1976 1978 The Muslim Institute
Croom Helm Ltd, 2-10 St John's Road, London SW11

British Library Cataloguing in Publication Data

Badawi, Zaki,
  The Reformers of Egypt.
  1. Islam and social problems — Egypt —
  History 2. Egypt — Social conditions
  I. Title
  301.24'2'0962   HN786

  ISBN 0-85664-651-2

Printed in Great Britain by Biddles Ltd, Guildford, Surrey

CONTENTS

PREFACE

Since these chapters were written some years ago, many significant works bearing on the subject have been published. But I found little reason to alter my presentation or analysis. The most important addition to our knowledge concerns the early life of Jamal Al-Din Al-Afghani,[1] whose Iranian origin has now been firmly and perhaps finally established. But I had little interest in Al-Afghani's biography. There is no doubt that the portrait of Al-Afghani based on factual documents is a most valuable contribution but need not make us change our view of him or adduce to him less honourable motives or regard him as a political trickster without loyalty to anything except agitation and disorder. We must attempt to understand his dilemma. A born Shi'i who has the vision of uniting the fragmented *Ummah* has the choice of proclaiming his call in his stark Shi'i colours only to be cruelly dismissed by the narrow-minded Sunnis of the thirteenth century A.H. Alternatively, he could declare his conversion to Sunnism as a prelude to his call for unity but if the Sunnis believed his conversion to be genuine, his call to unity with the Shi'is would be bound to arouse their suspicion. You do not seek such recognition for the creed you have just discarded. Further, it would not be logical to expect the Shi'is to answer his call to unity when he had just defected from their ranks. The only course open to Al-Afghani was the one he took in claiming to have been born a Sunni. What he did in this matter, given his aims and aspirations, is not abhorrent to Muslim Law or ethics.

My standpoint in writing these chapters was (and still is) that Islam is the true and final revelation of Allah. It is the straight path, but it is a broad path with many parallel lanes all springing from the same source and leading to the same destination. This view of Islam is derived from the Prophet who advised his companions to be tolerant and not opt for the difficult and rigid rules, thinking them to be more

7

pious for being more painful.[2] This allowed for the absorption and assimilation of many diverse cultures and civilisations by Islam. The end result was the greatest of all civilisations, the civilisation of Islam. This view of Islamic civilisation might appear as a large claim. The fruits of modern science and technology appear to make life so much more comfortable and work so much less arduous. This leads some to argue that we live and experience the 'greatest of all civilisations'.

But we must compare civilisations in all their manifestations and not only in one or two limited aspects. If the aim of human organisation is the achievement of happiness, then Islam will be found as having provided for contentment without passivity, for reliance on Allah without destroying human initiative or undervaluing human action. A happy civilisation is a great civilisation. Power, wealth and skill can be instruments of happiness and can also be tools of misery. Let those who admire modern technology be content with the destruction it has brought upon man and his environment. Let those who appreciate the high standard of physical health brought about by modern medicine lament the low standard of mental health brought about by the pressures of industrialisation.

Modern man might have been able to conquer the moon and probe the planets but he has not been able to conquer his own doubts, his place in the world, his ethical values and even the value of his life itself.

The empty temples of the discarded gods of the 'civilised world' have been replaced by vulgar shrines where physical pleasure and material wealth are held supreme. Fear of ultimate retribution is minimal and hope for final salvation has given way to despair. Is it any wonder then that the most powerful civilisation is also one of the most unhappy? No, I stick to my claim that Islam's is the greatest civilisation. Should Islam absorb and assimilate the modern civilisation, the result would be a civilisation with power restrained by ethical values, and wealth justly distributed by religious law and pleasure circumscribed by moral standards. This is the obvious role of Islam in the next phase of history and this, also, is the challenge that confronts the Muslims as they approach the end of the fourteenth century of the *Hijra*.

As mankind proceeds inexorably towards the next crisis of civilisation, a whole range of new institutions will be needed to give direction to change and stability to a fundamentally unstable situation. One of these is the Muslim Institute for Research and Planning which a band of dedicated founder members from all parts of the world is trying to establish with that very purpose in mind. I am glad to be one. The views expressed here are, of course, all mine.

I pray to Allah to guide mankind into the *sirat al-mustaqeem — Ameen*!

ZB

NOTES

1. See for instance the important publications of Professor Nikki Kiddi.
2. The Prophet is reported as having said, 'The Religion [of Islam] is the easy not the difficult way.'

INTRODUCTION

Modern Muslim thought emerged as a reaction to the impact of the West upon Muslim society. The West forced its way into the Dar Al-Islam, interfering in its affairs and reshaping its destiny. The initial reaction of the Muslims consisted in fortifying themselves with Western weaponry. It soon, however, became clear that a modern army presupposed a modern society. The age of the savage fighter descending upon the civilised world to ravage and plunder was over. Military power became one of the dimensions of the degree of modernity.

The influence of the West stemmed from the example of the victor whose culture and system of values carry the prestige of the overlord. But even more important than the Western example was modernity. The accumulation of knowledge has become institutionalised. Research laboratories and universities are driven by an unsatiated curiosity to discover and invent. It no longer responds solely to human needs. It invents them. But modernity, having grown in the Western environment, has been stamped with its own characteristic colour. There was naturally confusion in the minds of the Muslims as to what constituted progress and what was specifically Western. The distinction between the West and modernity, and consequently Westernisation and modernisation, became blurred. The Westernisers took it for granted that to be modern the Muslim community must be Western. The way to progress was assumed to be one way — the Western way.

As the confrontation between the West and the Muslim world was one between enemies of long historical standing, and as the Muslims faced modernity not gradually and piecemeal but in a highly developed form, their reaction was somewhat uncertain. Even more unsettling for Muslims was the continuous development arising from modernity, allowing for little time to adjust and react. The experience of the Muslims in relation to Hellenism was hardly helpful in

11

solving the new crisis. The problem caused by the impact of Hellenistic thought arose during a period of strength and independence. It confronted the Muslims with a static set of principles to incorporate, and it allowed the Muslims to accept or reject them. All these aspects were absent in its confrontation with modernity. Muslim society of the twelfth to thirteenth (eighteenth and nineteenth) centuries was weak and decadent. More importantly, it was not allowed to ignore such a powerful force (modernity) which impinged on the physical as well as on the intellectual and social environment of man. Adjustment to modernity thus took the form sometimes of accepting or adopting Western solutions before formulating specifically Muslim solutions stemming from Muslim culture and taking into account the Muslim system of values.

It was against the background of Westernisation that the reform school emerged. Its main aim was to provide solutions to allay Muslim conscience and permit Muslims to adopt and partake in Western scientific development. It was in a sense a resistance to European cultural penetration, and in another it was a yielding to what was considered science and technology. The distinction between the two aspects was never completely clear and the reformers sometimes accepted Western cultural values on the assumption that they constituted modernity. Yet it was this particular problem which aroused the strongest controversy in the Muslim world. Those who opposed change called every departure from the old tradition Westernisation, that is imitation of the hated enemy, the infidel West. Those who supported change called every aspect of it modernisation, however irrelevant the particular innovation might be to the needs of man in the scientific and technological age. The problem arising from this controversy touched upon theology, ethics, law and education. And because of the encroachment of the West on the political set-up of the Muslim society, political issues became also involved.

Modernity grew out of the environment dominated by the nation-state, by ideas of liberalism, individuality and limitations of the power of the authorities. The Muslims were quick to notice that and, like their Western contemporaries, to consider such institutions as parliament and all the trappings of Western political systems as in themselves the necessary dimensions of an advanced society.

The first Egyptian Muslim to perceive the importance of these institutions was Rifa'a Al-Tahtawi who regarded them as good, though not contained in the Shari'a. It is important to note that Tahtawi was hardly a supporter of democracy. His advocacy of the French institutions of parliament and constitution, etc. did not stem from any idea of limiting the powers of the executive. A generation later these institutions were made by the reformists a part of the Islamic political system, and ever since some Muslim writers and apologists have come to equate *Shura* with parliament, and *Bay'ah* with election. Thus Western institutions were *internalised* within the theoretical structure of the Islamic reform movement in Egypt.

Islamic reform was only one of many reactions that emanated from the *Ummah* in response to the challenge of European civilisation. There were at least four other distinctive reactions ranging from extreme conservatism to extreme Westernism. Perhaps it might help determine the place of the reform school if an outline of the other reactions is given:

1. The conservative reaction favours the *status quo* of the Muslims and abhors change in whatever form and under whatever banner. The upholders of this view are those scholars who accept the works of some authors (generally belonging to the eighth and ninth centuries (A. H.) as the final and unquestionable authority on Islam. Any deviation from their stated opinion is regarded as a deviation from Islam itself.

   The *Ummah*, the conservatives declare, should not be drawn away from the true path by the false Christian civilisation or the enticing arguments of those misguided Muslims who claim for themselves the right and ability to present other ideas about Islam. The door of *ijtihad*, they contend, is firmly closed because on the one hand no one is qualified for it any more and on the other there is no need for it. The authoritative books in use contain all the satisfactory answers to all the *valid* questions.

Central to this outlook is the view that modern civil-isation is false and transient. It will go away of its own accord so why tamper with the eternal message of Islam for the sake of an unreal and ephemeral civilisation.

Thus, in the field of ideas and emotional commitment, they think and argue and feel as if the world around them had remained static since their chosen author had finally concluded the last paragraph of his work. In real life, however, they live and act like all of their contemporaries.

Included in this category (the conservatives) are some — though not all — Sufi leaders whose doctrine rejects this world and advocates withdrawal from it into the eternal reality. To withdraw from the unpleasantness of this world rather than seek to change it is tantamount to accepting or at least tolerating it as it is, i.e. conserving it.

2. The Westernising reaction is on the other extreme. It is for the total acceptance of Western culture along with the adoption of science and technology. This view is best expressed in the words of Taha Husain: 'Let us adopt Western civilisation in its totality and all its aspects, the good with the bad and the bitter with the sweet.' Funda-mental to this outlook is the conviction that 'progress' rather than religion is what matters. Religion is, therefore, relegated to the limited sphere of relation between man the individual and his chosen deity. Thus Islam, in this view, is equated with all other religions and doctrines as one of manifold forms of belief systems which may exist, but need not significantly influence the march to 'civili-sation'.

3. Close to this viewpoint but somewhat different from it is that of the Muslim secularists. They subscribe to the goal of the modernists, viz, that the legitimate aspiration of the *Ummah* is that of civilisation and progress. They differ, however, in claiming that their view is based not on the intrinsic value of 'civilisation and progress' but on Islam itself. When the secularist Ali Abdul-Razik pro-

claimed that the Caliphate was a secular, not a religious, institution and that the political, judicial and economic activities of the Muslims should be guided by their worldly interests unfettered by religious consideration, he was applauded by every Westerniser. But he went further and bestowed on his opinion the authority of Islam itself.

He thus introduced an interpretation of Islamic history and doctrines at variance with the accepted view and proceeded to proclaim that every one was wrong – presumably including the Companions – in believing that Islam aimed at further than the uplift of man's spiritual life and moral values. As for the mundane aspects of society, he stated, they were too trivial to be of concern to Allah's revelation.

Neither the Westerniser nor the secularist succeeded in gaining much ground within the ranks of the *Ummah*. Their ideas were rejected but their programme was, however, implemented. The Muslim communities – with few exceptions – live at present under secular governments administering imported 'civilised' systems of law and forming a part of a European-dominated economic system. The disparity between the ideal of the *Ummah* and the actuality could not be more glaring or more agonising. To bridge this gap the revivalists came on the scene.

4. The revivalist or revolutionary reaction proclaims that the ills of the *Ummah* cannot be remedied except by reference back to Islam in its purity as represented by Al-Qur'an and the Prophetic Traditions. It might be argued that revivalism should not be categorised as a modern reaction to a contemporary challenge since Muslim history is punctuated by revivalist movements emerging as a result of internal factors rather than external threats.

While not denying that the dynamic nature of Islam brings forth from time to time movements of revival to check the drift of the *Ummah* from the straight path, there is no doubting the fact that the modern revivalists focused most of their effort on exorcising the pernicious influence of modern civilisation. The reader can test this claim by glancing at the works of some of the modern revivalists such as Hassan al-Banna of Egypt, Maududi of Pakistan, Muhammad Natsir of Indonesia and Burhanussin Al-Hilmi of Malaya.

The revivalists aim at re-establishing Islam in its totality through persuasion, if possible, or force, if necessary. Hence the emphasis on the duty of *jihad* and the repeated allusions to the early days of Islam with all the sacrifices and struggles that preceded the final triumph. In contrast with the reformists, the Westernisers and the secularists, the revivalists are a mass movement, confident in the Divine source of its belief and certain of the final victory of its Faith.

Although the revivalists sought to stem the tide of Westernisation, and naturally incurred the hostility of the Westerniser and the secularists, they have not in the process gained the confidence or the support of the conservatives. In fact the struggle between the conservatives and the revivalists was often more bitter and deadly than with any other group. The reason can be found in the fact that they both seek to control the masses.

In the circumstances of the *Ummah* divided as it is into nation-states, the political leadership in nearly all of them remains for the moment in the hands of Westernisers of whatever variety. The revivalists are generally ignored as long as they are few and unsuccessful but once they assume the leadership of the masses, the secular authorities bring to bear upon them the might of the Westernised state.

The reformists, though they are, as Ridha described them, the party of the few, are of great significance in modern Muslim thought. They represent a form of synthesis of various trends within the *Ummah* and their influence is much greater than their number warrants.

The Westerniser and secularists sometimes claim to be the natural heirs of the reformists while some revivalists, such as Hassan Al-Banna, were in certain respects a continuation of Ridha, the reformist.

It must, however, be pointed out that these categories are points on a continuum stretching from extreme conservatism to extreme Westernism. The place of a thinker on this continuum is determined by his views on a majority of the important issues. Few, if any, hold the same attitude on all issues and it is therefore possible for one and the same person to be conservative with regard to a particular question while being almost a Westerniser in relation to another and still a reformist in connection with yet another question. This observation must be borne in mind when assessing the views of the reformists in particular. By the nature of their stand they seem the least consistent, as the middle course is the most elusive.

In the following pages we deal with the views of three major leaders of the Reform School in Egypt. Jamal Al-Din Al-Afghani, Muhammad 'Abduh and Rashid Ridha. The first was the Socrates of the movement. He wrote little but inspired a great deal. It is difficult to be certain, with regard to the early contributions of 'Abduh, what emanated from Al-Afghani and what was exclusively 'Abduh's. The relationship between 'Abduh and Ridha is even more complex, especially when it is realised that Ridha sometimes read into 'Abduh's thought what was entirely his own.

1 JAMAL AL-DIN AL-AFGHANI

The epithet of the 'Awakener of the East' with which Rashid Ridha often prefaces the name of al-Afghani is probably an exaggeration. He, however, was not alone in attributing to Al-Afghani a major role in the disturbed reaction of the Muslim world to European expansion in the last quarter of the nineteenth century.[1] That he influenced or associated himself with all the important developments in countries as widely separated as India and Egypt, the Sudan and Iran is well known. He was able through political activity, skilful propaganda and an unusual understanding of European expansionist designs to assume such a position *vis-à-vis* Europe that most colonial powers watched him with apprehension and some even sought an understanding with him.[2] It is nevertheless important that we should bear in mind that the movement of ideas with which Al-Afghani's name is so closely associated had its genesis in Muslim countries well before he appeared on the scene. Had he never existed, someone would most certainly have come forward to play the role. It was merely the formulation of the problem and the forceful articulation of the solutions that bore the stamp of his powerful personality. He was a born leader. His genius manifested itself not so much in the sphere of ideas as in the correct analysis of a situation and identifying himself with the most plausible and acceptable trend.

Important though he is for the historian of Muslim thought and Muslim revolutionary movements, his life remains full of obscurities. Many gaps are still to be filled, and most of our information about him was supplied by himself. Corroborating evidence for his information had not always been available. He remains historically a shadowy figure. Politically and intellectually he is a vivid force.[3]

Al-Afghani first visited Egypt in about 1869 where he stayed for some forty days on his way to Istanbul. Though he was then, according to his own account a political refugee, he was announced as a man of great learning from Afghanistan.[4] After a short stay in Istanbul, he was expelled in consequence of a dispute between him and the Shaikh Al-Islam. It appeared that Al-Afghani treated prophecy in a way that provoked the animosity of religious officials. There seem also to have been other personal reasons.[5]

Riadh Pasha, the Chief Minister of Egypt, invited Al-Afghani to stay in Egypt; and without specifying any duties for him he granted him ten thousand piastres a month. No doubt Riadh Pasha, like many of the progressive Turks in Istanbul, was greatly impressed by Al-Afghani and must have assumed that the presence of such a great teacher would be of cultural value to Egypt. Al-Afghani fulfilled this promise, for he gathered around him many students, government officials and intellectuals of varying calibre and instilled his ideas into them. He further held regular courses in philosophy, logic and higher theology in his own residence for a number of admiring students. He also encouraged his students to disseminate his ideas through the press and he was at least partially responsible for the appearance of a newspaper of opinion which became his mouthpiece.[6] But this was not the limit of Al-Afghani's activities. His restless personality, sharp intelligence and violent temperament were not wholly suited to the contemplative tasks of the scholar.

The deterioration of government under Isma'il, the growth of European influence and the collapse of Egypt's economy combined to create for the first time in the history of modern Egypt a public opinion against the government. The traditional attitude which makes obedience to the ruler a manifestation of obedience to Allah no longer held in Egypt. Everyone was trying to find a way to salvation. Isma'il was now completely without friends. But more important than the destiny of the ruler was the destiny of the system itself. Muhammad 'Ali's greatly centralised government was now failing and an alternative was being desperately sought. There was a strong current of opinion that Isma'il's failures resulted from absolute power and that the remedy would be to limit the powers of the ruler. As many of the leading intellectuals and politicians in Egypt at that time were French-educated, the French model of constitutional government proved to them very attractive. These 'constitutionalists',[7] under the leadership of Sharif Pasha, had their faces firmly turned towards Europe, or more specifically France.

They operated under the misapprehension that Europe's progress was due to the form of its government. Seldom, if ever, did they suspect that governmental institutions reflected social forces within the society. Al-Afghani appeared to have been among the few who were fully aware of this fact.[8] As events grew more confusing and dangerous, Al-Afghani suspended his regular lessons presumably to devote his time to political intrigue.[9] At this stage he conducted a campaign through the press and public speeches to expose Isma'il and demolish whatever little prestige his government still had.[10] It is significant that neither Al-Afghani nor his students spoke as Muslims. His writings and those of his chief disciple reflect nationalist and sometimes racialist rather than specifically Muslim inspiration.[11] He further betrayed a hatred for Britain that was to characterise most of his activities. In his opinion Great Britain constituted the gravest menace to Islam and in combating her ambitions he was willing to enlist the support of France, Russia or any other force available.[12]

His main preoccupation was external defence, but he realised that it could best be achieved through internal reform. External threat, he reasoned, was brought about by European superior techniques. 'The Oriental Question', he said to *Makhzumi,* 'would never have existed had the Ottomans matched the West in the field of civilisation and coupled its material conquests with scientific power.'[13]

The visible military threat from the West figures very largely in Egyptian horizons. Al-Afghani was very conscious of the dangers inherent in the situation in the late 1870s, and like many others thought reforms were necessary, but he was uncertain as to the specific nature of these reforms. In his conversations with Makhzumi he recalled how he expressed his doubts about the value of a legislative assembly unless it emerged from the people themselves. 'An assembly brought forth at the behest of a king, prince or a foreign power . . . its authority will be illusory and dependent on the will of its creator.'[14] He nevertheless advised Tawfiq that he should 'hasten to make the nation participate in government

... and should order an election to choose representatives to legislate.' This Al-Afghani suggested 'would be a strength to the throne and give permanence to your authority'.[15]

This confusion between advocating a particular system of government and doubting its suitability for the Orientals may have been a reflection of Al-Afghani's own inability to reconcile constitutional government with the precepts of Islam. It may on the other hand indicate certain authoritarian tendencies on his part, for his famous article on absolute government calls not for a representative, democratic government but for an enlightened dictatorship.[16] The positive contents of Al-Afghani's politics are always ill-defined. Although he regarded the republican form of government (al-Hukumat al-Jumhuriyyah) as the highest,[17] he was still willing to support an enlightened dictator.[18] He, however, brought to Egyptian politics two fundamental concepts; the first is that rulership was not the privilege of a particular race and was not unconditional;[19] the second was that a ruler's retention of power is contingent on his performing his duties.[20] In the quietistic and submissive Egyptian society these ideas were extremely revolutionary and if a few years after Al-Afghani's departure from Egypt an Egyptian fellah could stand in front of the Khedive and say, 'We are born free,'[21] it was in no small measure due to Al-Afghani's revolutionary agitation.[22] Al-Afghani extended his views into international politics and was perhaps the first Oriental in modern times to reject the idea of European supremacy. Fundamental to his activities and agitation was his conviction that the imperial system was of a temporary duration.[23] It was for this reason among others that he attacked Sir Ahmad Khan so severely[24] and expressed his astonishment at the failure of 'Abduh to expel the British from Egypt after he returned from exile.[25]

The biographers may differ about many things concerning Al-Afghani, but one thing they all agree upon is that he unswervingly opposed British colonialism. His booklet on the relations between Britain and Afghanistan[26] expressed his views with vehemence. *Al 'Urwat al Wuthqa* was another and more violent expression of his enmity towards British colonialism. In a sense his hatred for the colonial system constituted the motive force in his life.[27] He decried European expansion as immoral and unjust because of the violence that was its basis. 'The English', he said to Makhzumi, 'deny the wealth of India to the Indians. They take it as their own simply because the Indians are weaker than themselves.'[28] Because he regarded Europe of the nineteenth century as unjust he declined to describe it as civilised.

> All the scientific gains and whatever good these [Western] nations' civilisation, if weighed against the wars and sufferings they cause, these scientific gains would undoubtedly prove to be too little and the wars and sufferings too great. Such a progress, civilisation and science in this fashion and with these results are undiluted ignorance, sheer barbarism and total savagery. Man in this respect is lower than animal.[29]

This strong indictment however is not carried to the point of complete pacifism. Like the good theologian he was, he found war objectionable only if it was unjust or unnecessarily cruel.

In other words he was moved not by humanitarian sentiments but by religious dogma. In his view there was a fundamental distinction between Muslim and European expansion both in manner and purpose; the latter lacked the humane and gentle attitude towards adversaries of the former. Further, European conquests were motivated by greed and sustained by oppression and deceit. In contrast, Muslim drives against their neighbours were to free the people from tyranny and to allow them unhampered access to the message of Allah.[30]

His activities must have attracted the secret services of the colonial powers. Statesmen and thinkers took note of his ideas as he grew in importance through the newspapers he helped to create.[31] There is no doubt that he attempted an understanding with the various colonial powers on issues of importance to Islam. The report suggesting that he offered himself for the British Secret Service must, however, be regarded with extreme scepticism.[32]

If his political standing against the British is clear and

unequivocal, his religious conviction has been doubted by many scholars. His contemporaries among the conservative *ulema* accused him of heresy.[33] But as the nature of orthodoxy changed and liberal ideas penetrated deeply into Muslim society Al-Afghani became more acceptable, indeed, he proved a hero. Doubts about his conviction nevertheless remained supported by a few Muslims and many Orientalists.[34]

Suspicions concerning Al-Afghani's convictions stemmed from various sources. His enemies in Istanbul, namely Hassan Effendi the Shaikh Al Islam, accused him in 1869/70 of heresy concerning his exposition of prophecy. 'Abduh considered the views of Al-Afghani on this issue to be in accordance with orthodoxy. The Prophet was the spirit which completed the happiness of man in society.[35] A. M. Goichon contradicts this view in suggesting that Al-Afghani deviated from orthodoxy in emphasising the utilitarian function of prophecy.[36]

Elie Kedourie[37] bases his arguments largely on circumstantial evidence and guilt by association. His contribution to the discussion is his emphasis on the general trend in Muslim élite circles of speaking to the masses with different tongues and different symbols and on the fact that despotic rule in the Orient did not permit of freedom of expression. N. R. Keddie goes further[38] in calling upon the Persian environment which she supposed to form the background of Al-Afghani with its traditional scepticism among the intellectuals to throw further doubt on Al-Afghani. In another work[39] she promised to show that Al-Afghani's *Al-Radd Ala Al Dahriyyin* (*Refutation of the Materialists*) has in fact a double meaning and could be read and understood differently by the élite and the mass of the people.

Amidst all these accusations one point had to be accounted for, namely the unbounded energy and enthusiasm of Al-Afghani for the cause he claimed as his own. A. Hourani, holding the opposite viewpoint, observes[40] that Al-Afghani 'not only believed that Islam was as true or false as other religions, but that it was the one true, complete and perfect religion'. Such a belief appears essential as a motive force for Al-Afghani's life and work. It is difficult to explain his activity in terms of purely political ambition. There are so many things and many episodes in his life that could not be accounted for in this fashion.[41] Doubts stemming from his statements, however, cannot be disregarded simply as false interpretation, nor can these statements be twisted to accord with his other and more acceptable ones, except at the expense of either language or common sense.[42]

It appears that insincerity is not an adequate explanation for Al-Afghani's work, nor can the near sainthood conferred upon him by Rashid Ridha explain fully the inconsistencies in Al-Afghani's life and statements. In the view of this writer, Al-Afghani was consistent with regard to one overriding emotion and loyalty. He conceived of himself as a member of a community with Islam as the base of its culture and facing the same destiny as the rest of the 'Orient'. In this sense Al-Afghani did not have to have a strong belief in Islam as a religion, nor necessarily address the public with regard to his real beliefs. This is not to accuse him of insincerity, for it is my view that he was completely and utterly sincere. He was cast in the role of the Muslim Oriental by nineteenth-century Europe with all the implications of cultural backwardness and racial inferiority. Not surprisingly, he clashed over these two issues with Renan, the first European thinker to give intellectual formulation to prevailing prejudices.[43] The effect of Europe experienced at first hand by Al-Afghani was to strengthen his attachment to the *Ummah* and probably shake his faith still further. His overt statements were motivated by the first tendency whereas his private and restricted utterances or writings may have represented the second. His article in *Abu Naddara* and *Al-Basir*,[44] together with *Al'Urwat al Wuthqa*, manifested the former whereas his rejoinder to Renan was not meant for the general public. There is no reason for us to surmise as regards this. In a recently uncovered letter written by 'Abduh to Al-Afghani, 'Abduh says,

We were informed before the arrival of your letter about what was published in *Le Journal des Débats* by yourself in defence of Islam (and what a defence!) in reply to Monsieur Renan. We thought it one of those religious

triflings [sic] which would find acceptance on the part of
the believers. We urged one of those religious ones to
translate it. But the issues of *Le Journal des Débats* were
not (Praise be to Allah) available to us till the arrival of
your letter. We perused the two issues translated to us by
Hassan Effendi Bayham. We consequently dissuaded our
first friend from translating it and we used in this respect a
promise to give him the Arabic origin of the article which
we told him would be coming and then published, and
therefore no reason for translation. *Thus what we feared
was avoided.*[45]

This significant letter, which was either suppressed by Rashid
Ridha or more likely was kept from him by 'Abduh, confirms our interpretation of Al-Afghani's attitude. It continues
as follows:

We are at present following your straight path (the head of
religion is cut off only with the sword of religion) if you
therefore saw us you would see ascetics continuously
worshipping, bending and prostrating, never disobeying
God in what He orders them and doing what they ordered.
'Without hope, life would be unbearable.'

This confirms the suggestion that both Al-Afghani and 'Abduh
may have been less conformist than many of their admirers
would like, but we need not accept the views of their detrac-
tors who depict them as mere charlatans, motivated purely
by political ambitions. There is no doubt in my mind that
both Al-Afghani and 'Abduh believed in the superiority of
Islamic culture and Islam as religion over all other religions.
It must be noted that both 'Abduh and Al-Afghani stressed
the cultural side of Islam at the expense of the purely theological.

Far more important than the actuality of his belief is the
image he built for himself, or was built for him throughout
the Muslim world. Whether he was a Sunni Afghan or a
Shi'i Persian or a sceptic, his influence remains powerful and
as the colonial era declines, his views become vindicated. The
Muslim nations who would like to document their real or

imagined resistance to the encroachment of Europe may seek consciously or unconsciously to inflate the image of Al-Afghani and to magnify his contribution.[46] It is significant that in recent years several biographies of him have been published in the Arabic language, and that many editions of his most famous works, namely *Al 'Urwat al Wuthqa* and *Al Radd 'ala al Dahriyyin* have also appeared. His reputation, which was largely posthumous,[47] continues to grow, stifling all criticism and calling for nothing less than a scholarly study of his life's work.[48]

The name of Al-Afghani is closely associated with the Pan-Islamic Movement which flourished in the last quarter of the nineteenth century and the early years of the twentieth century. There is no doubt that Al-Afghani, at least when he was in Europe, was working for the unity of the Muslim world under the Caliph.[49] He was, however, enough of a realist to appreciate the difficulty of Muslims coming under one rule. He therefore suggested that the Muslims need not be united in one single state but could achieve such a unity as essential for their defence. In other words, Al-Afghani suggested unity in foreign policy and defence.[50] 'Abduh's denial of Pan-Islamism being a policy of Al-Afghani belongs to a different period, and as shown below, was aimed at placating the anger of militant Europe. Unity in itself was not the aim of Al-Afghani. It was a means to an end, namely to the realisation of Islam's position in the world *vis-à-vis* its major enemy — the Christian West.[51]

But to deal with Europe necessitated the learning of the secret of its power and adopting the instruments of its military strength. Thus Al-Afghani was calling not only for the discarding of internal disputes but also for dismantling of the barriers which kept the Muslims unable or unwilling to partake in science and technology. These two proposals have far-reaching consequences. In the first place, the insistence of unity meant either the discarding or the radical re-interpretation of Muslim history. Al-Afghani chose to re-interpret Muslim history and to attribute differences between the Shi'a and the Sunni to the machinations of kings.[52] But this was, to say the least, an oversimplification, yet Al-Afghani was bent on achieving unity between the Shah and the Caliph, and he formulated an outline of an agreement between them upon which it appears that he was invited to Istanbul.[53]

To re-interpret the history of a religion is to re-interpret the religion itself, and Al-Afghani was led into the position of advocating a new Ijtihad and the discarding of the authority of the established scholars. Their opinions, he contended, are not binding upon us. The aim of the new Ijtihad is to arrive at the true Islam, the Islam which is not corrupted by harmful ideas and practices. Thus Al-Afghani, while adopting the call of the Wahhabis, 'Let us go back to the Qur'an and the Tradition,' twisted it into 'Let us modernise our society to compete on equal terms with the West.' In other words, he agreed with the Wahhabis in decrying the innovations of the Middle Ages but he did not decry innovations as such, for it was one of his major aims to renovate Muslim society.

In advocating a new Ijtihad, Al-Afghani hit at the base of nineteenth-century Islam and the general concept Muslims had of themselves. He could no longer accept the position current in his time of fatalism and the inevitable deterioration of mankind. He rejected most firmly the concept of man as a feather in the wind and insisted that he is capable of influencing events and deciding his destiny.[54] He also advocated the idea that man can strive for perfection and claimed that Islam provides him with the social system best suited to help him achieve this task.[55]

But if Islam was the religion best suited to progress, why should the Muslims be less progressive than their contemporaries? Al-Afghani found the answer in analysing Muslim history. He ascribed the causes of Muslim decline to the corruption and alterations introduced by the Sufis, the *Zindiqs,* the Sophists and those who fabricated the sayings of the Prophet. Through all these the concept of Islam as a fatalistic, backward-looking religion without social responsibility and with a strong objection to activity and ambition was developed.[56]

Al-Afghani regarded Islam as the essential basis for the progress of Muslims. It was vital, therefore, that Islam itself should present not only neutrality towards progress but a positive encouragement of it. For this purpose the presentation of Islam must be in terms of civilisation rather than theology. Similarly, the attack on the religion of Islam must be regarded as an attack aimed at the very existence of the *Ummah*. He saw a conspiracy against the *Ummah* not only in the attacks of missionaries and priests, but also in the pro-Western modernism of Sir Sayyid Ahmad Khan.[57] He observes that those Muslims who renounce Islam, unlike the anti-religious Europeans, lose their allegiance to their countries and to their nation, thus making it easier for the foreigner to dominate them.[58] The call for a new Ijtihad and for striving towards perfection meant that the community must discard its lethargy and take part in the struggle for progress. A Muslim Reformation was, in his view, necessary for achieving this.[59] He often mentioned Luther and attributed to his movement the success of Europe and felt that a similar Reformation would rejuvenate Islam and set the Ummah on the road to progress.[60] Beyond these broad principles Al-Afghani seldom ventured. He avoided discussing detailed programmes, whether because of his intellectual limitations[61] or because the task he set for himself demanded evoking the emotional response for the general principles as a prelude to the more reasoned attitude for the detailed programme[62] is difficult to ascertain.

Al-Afghani wanted to reform Islam, not to modernise it.[63] He proposed to the *Ummah* that it should base its progress on its own religion and its own Qur'an.[64] If he rejected imitating the ancient Muslim scholars, he was as firm in rejecting imitating the modern European.[65] He was contemptuous of those who adopt the customs of other nations, and regarded them as a menace to the security of the nation.[66] This was his final Pan-Islamic phase. In his early career in Egypt, as has already been observed, he spoke in terms of nationalism and, according to Rashid Ridha, formed a nationalist party and addressed the masses of Egyptians as 'Amhouri, reportedly alluding to race rather than religion.[67] Al-Afghani, like 'Abduh, believed that the use of religion as the basis for reform and progress was essential, even inevitable, in the Muslim society. If religion is the base upon which reform is to be built, it follows inevitably that the adoption of new measures and new ideas must accord with the basic principles of Islam. In other words, Islam rather than any other social system must be the measure against which reform is to be valued. This amongst other things was an important distinction between him and Sir Sayyid Ahmad Khan.[68]

His dispute with Ahmad Khan, coming so soon after his expulsion from Egypt and his 'conversion' to Pan-Islamism, was prompted by the political implications of Khan's programme. Al-Afghani, however, went beyond the limits of intelligent discussion and accused Ahmad Khan, without as it appears reading any of his works, of heresy as well as treason. In the work which was written in reply to a question about Ahmad Khan's ideas, Al-Afghani chose to discuss the ideas of all the 'materialists' from Ancient Greek to nineteenth-century philosophers but without reference to the ideas of Ahmad Khan. In *Al 'Urwat al Wuthqa* his references to Ahmad Khan are both erroneous and venomous.[69] It is true that Ahmad Khan's ideas may lead to the 'dethronement of God'[70] but, as Al-Afghani well knew, religious ideas are not measured by their implications, only by their direct statements. Al-Ghazali in his most restrictive phase did not brand either the Mu'tazila or the Philosophers as Kafirs for their adherence to the principles of causality.[71]

The function of religion, as Al-Afghani saw it was to instil in the human soul the basis of human society and civilisation and the motive force to drive 'the peoples and tribes towards progress to the limits of perfection'.[72] Religion, he suggests, instils in the human soul the conviction that man is the noblest creature and that one's nation is the noblest of nations and that man came into this world to achieve perfection to prepare him for ascendance into a world more noble and embracing than this.[73] He felt that these beliefs influence moral behaviour towards adherence to the accepted norms of society and towards honesty and truthfulness. He declares these to be essential to the survival of society and without which social conflict would be inevitable. He therefore sees materialism as a direct threat to the well-being of human society and is careful in his 'historical survey' of materialism to show its close association with decline and decadence.[74] He attributes to the belief in the Day of Judgement and in a transcendental being, the power to control human behaviour without which vice would be rife. He concludes his book with a section to prove that Islam is the greatest religion, and that it contained all these aspects which ensure the complete happiness of nations.[75] He believes these aspects to be the freedom of the mind from superstitions and the belief in oneself to be capable of reaching the highest degree of human perfection except that of prophethood, and that reason should be the basis of belief without imitation but through proper evidence. He quotes Guizot's *Histoire de la civilisation en Europe* as supporting the idea that European civilisation came about largely through the efforts of those with independent minds who claimed the right to question the basis of belief in Christianity and rejected the authority of religious officials. Al-Afghani also considered as a basis of civilisation the existence of a section of the population to guide the nation in the fields of knowledge and behaviour and another to educate and lead it to the ideal behaviour.[76]

In Al-Afghani's view the ideal state cannot be realised in this world except through Islam.[77] He promised to write an essay proving this point. It was an unfulfilled promise, just as his promise to write a theological (rather than sociological) refutation of the materialists was unfulfilled.[78] What significance is there for the failure of Al-Afghani to write these two essays? Is it because of lack of conviction or because, as observed earlier, of intellectual limitation?

In the realm of politics Al-Afghani was consistent in his opposition to British imperialism. He also decried absolute rule prevalent in the Muslim countries of his time; but he was no constitutionalist.[79] His inspiration appears to vacillate between liberal ideas common in the Francophile circles of Egypt and the traditional concepts of the ideal Muslim government. Whether this vacillation was due, as Ahmad Amin suggests, to his historical development[80] or to a lack of clarity in his positive programme is difficult to ascertain, though this writer is inclined to the second view. He rejected, as Ahmad Khan did, the nineteenth-century Islam and insisted that people must free themselves from Taqlid (blind imitation). To the suggestion that the door of Ijtihad was closed, he replied,

What does it mean? On the basis of what authority was it closed and which Imam said that no one after me should think independently in matters of religion or should derive guidance from the Qur'an, the authentic Tradition, deduction through analogy in accordance with modern science and the needs of the age and its contingencies?[81]

He declared that 'Religion should not contradict scientific facts. If it appeared to do so then it must be re-interpreted.' He decried the ignorant and rigid *ulema* of his day whose attitude led to the accusation that the Qur'an contradicts the established scientific facts, 'but the Qur'an is innocent of what they say and the Qur'an must be regarded as too noble to contradict scientific facts especially with regard to general principles'.[82] He even went further and claimed that the Qur'an contains references to scientific discoveries which can only be seen once human knowledge arrives at them.[83] Perhaps this claim was the origin of the trend towards scientific exegesis of the Qur'an, as Tantawi Jawhari attempted later.

But the rebellion against traditional Islam disguised as an attack on blind imitation has as a conscious aim the breaking up of the exclusiveness of Muslim society to allow for greater unity among Muslims and co-operation with non-Muslims for their common interest. Al-Afghani therefore advocated the unity of Sunni and Shi'i Muslims and also the unity of all Orientals *vis-à-vis* Europe. This was the phase after his expulsion from Egypt characterised by his efforts in *Al Urwat Al Wuthqa* and also his writings in India.[84] He regarded religion *per se,* especially the three Semitic religions (Judaism, Christianity and Islam) as not a dividing factor. It becomes so only through the professionals with their vested interests.[85] If he sought to break the exclusiveness of Muslim society and open up its boundaries to new influences and new alliances, he was not calling for less than a transformation of the mentality of the people of his day and the change in the social system to allow for greater flexibility and movement within the society from one class to another and of the society from one stage of development to another. It is this principle of movement, action and development which characterises Al-Afghani's thought and life. He objected most strongly to the lethargy of nineteenth-century Muslims and refuted its theological foundation and portrayed Islam as synonymous with action.[86]

Al-Afghani's basic aim was resistance to Europe. His most important means was the awakening of the Muslims from slumbers of superstition and ignorance to partake in modern civilisation, especially science and technology. The battle against Europe consumed most of his time and effort at the expense of preparing the Muslim educationally and socially. The teacher in him gave way to the politician, or, in the words of Rashid Ridha, Al-Afghani 'was a theologian overcome by politics'.[87] It led him into a tacit alliance with the French (he did not refer to their colonial conquests) who allowed him to use Paris as the headquarters of his secret society and the home of his publication. Its suspension within eighteen months must be attributed to the British either cutting off its financial resources in India and Egypt or else to their success in persuading the French to stop its publication.[88] His departure to Russia and long sojourn there was probably connected with the growing interest of the Czar in India and the approaches to its borders through Afghanistan. His appearance later in Western Europe and meetings with the Shah and travels to Persia and his expulsion from there are episodes reflecting his fluctuating fortunes. Though he might have been regarded by the rulers of his day as a man of exceptional ability, he was too much of a revolutionary to adjust to the system of his day. His objection to the Khedive, the Shah or the Sultan must have been much more than he cared to admit. He never succeeded in keeping an office for long. He always attempted to speak to the public over the heads of the rulers.

One point, however, must strike his biographers: that is his relation with the *ulema* of his day. In his Egyptian period he appeared to be contemptuous of them and incurred their enmity, especially the most conservative. In India, however, he allied himself with the conservatives, giving their case a modern twist. But in Europe he regarded the *ulema* as the pivot of his grand design. If Islam is to be the vehicle of rejuvenation and the weapon of resistance then its knights, the *ulema*, must be treated with care and during this period the *ulema* with their knowledge could be called upon to lead the people into battle against the invaders and against religious corruption. His call evoked little immediate action in Sunni circles. Among the Shi'ites, however, especially with reference to the tobacco incident, his agitation got immediate and positive response.[89] Although his stay in Persia during his active period was short, his influence remained immensely powerful and his followers not only murdered the Shah but were instrumental in propagating his ideas, which were not without influence in the 1905 Revolution. Was this because Al-Afghani was more able to speak to the Shi'i than to the Sunnis? Was it because his conduct and ideas conformed more with a Shi'i background than that of a Sunni 'alim of the nineteenth century, or was it because Al-Afghani's activities in the area of Perso-Afghanistan were those of the politician, whereas his activities in the Sunni world brought him into competition with its *ulema*?[90]

Though many aspects of Sir Sayyid Ahmad Khan's programme were acceptable to him, he objected to the political assumptions that lay behind it and may have suspected the theological foundations of the naturists.[91] He fully deserves the statement by Professor W. C. Smith: 'A very great deal of subsequent Islamic development is adumbrated in his personality and career. In fact, there is very little in twentieth-century Islam not foreshadowed in Al-Afghani.'[92] His legacy of resistance was carried later by the many nationalist leaders in Egypt and elsewhere. His programme for reform was elaborated by his disciple 'Abduh and carried by Rashid Ridha into wider and more detailed fields.

2 MUHAMMAD 'ABDUH

Al-Afghani's most important student was the Egyptian Azharite Muhammad 'Abduh. Like his teacher, 'Abduh perceived his task as attempting to bring Muslim society forward into the modern world. Also like his master, he appreciated the role of education, the importance of social organisation and the need to understand Islam in terms relevant to the conditions of the day. However, 'Abduh played a role that made him much more than a student of Al-Afghani.

After his exile from Egypt he joined Al-Afghani in 1882 in Paris, where they published the periodical *Al 'Urwat al Wuthqa* for the specific purpose of frustrating British policies in the Muslim world through uniting Islam against them. The political and religious views contained in this publication emanated from Al-Afghani[1] but it is certain that 'Abduh declared his disillusionment with political activities and was critical of Al-Afghani's preoccupation with them.[2] It is important to appreciate the true relationship between Al-Afghani and 'Abduh. Al-Afghani, a man of unbounded energy, unlimited ambitions, and above all a man untied to family or country, was naturally free to indulge in political intrigues that took him into many parts of the globe and made him a fugitive. His anchor was in his ideal of Muslim unity and his sometimes unrealistic optimism filled him with hope of achieving what all contemporary observers knew to be impossible. But Al-Afghani the revolutionary thrived on being always in opposition. His colourful, romantic personality, his message of hope, the role of the scholar fighter in which he cast himself attracted Muslims greatly to him. 'Abduh's fame, deriving no doubt through the activities of Rashid Ridha, was one of the windfalls of his association with Al-Afghani. Ridha declares openly that his attraction to 'Abduh was simply because he was the best available substitute for Al-Afghani.[3] Whenever he compares 'Abduh with Al-Afghani it is invariably to the disadvantage of the former.[4]

'Abduh, a peasant in origin, a family man and a practical and unadventurous person was ready to co-operate with the authorities. Extremism was never one of his traits except under the influence of Al-Afghani. He had all the peasant's attachment to the land of his origin and all the family man's desire for security. While he was a student and a colleague of Al-Afghani, he was completely influenced by him and, indeed, for a considerable period after the exile of Al-Afghani from Egypt in 1879 until the Urabi rebellion, Al-Afghani's influence was still powerful in 'Abduh's writings; yet 'Abduh exhibits the civil servant's care not to offend superiors.[5] When arrested after the British victory over Urabi in 1882 his defence was that he obeyed orders from his superiors throughout his work. Broadly, his English lawyer at the trial in Cairo found 'Abduh's claim completely confirmed.[6] It is this part of his character, his strong desire to associate himself with power that was both his greatest asset and most damaging weakness. He was able to be an associate of Al-Afghani, the revolutionary, and a supporter of Riadh Pasha, the gradualist reformer.

Once Riadh fell from power he found it easy to switch his allegiance to the revolutionary army officers, reversing all his arguments for gradualism and patience.[7] His quarrels with the army officers appear to have been motivated more by regard for the susceptibilities of the rulers than by the unfeasibility or otherwise of their programme. Once he was allowed back in Egypt he immediately made approaches to the real power in the country, namely Cromer. In a letter he wrote to Cromer on his arrival he openly offers his co-operation to combat 'fanaticism' and propagate the benefits of the Cromer régime through education.[8] He hoped that Cromer would help him obtain the principalship of Dar-Al-Ulum. What grounds must 'Abduh, the ex-chief editor of the most violent anti-British periodical, have had to make him hope that a British colonial administrator would entrust him with an influential educational office? It has been suggested that 'Abduh might have had to undertake not to interfere in politics before he was allowed to return to Egypt[9] but it is a strange way to interpret such an undertaking as meaning co-operation or even justification of the Cromer régime. No sooner was he in Egypt than it became known that he was popular with the British. His ability alone could not explain his meteoric rise in the judicial system.[10] Ability under the colonial system and especially under Cromer was the last criterion for advancement of Egyptians.[11] His fortune was assured and the nationalists never tired of accusing him of sacrificing everything for love of power. His reputed courage in standing up to Khedive Abbas in a trivial matter concerning Al Azhar is illusory. He as well as everybody else in Egypt was aware that Abbas was impotent *vis-à-vis* the protection of Cromer.[12] 'Abduh's co-operation with the British and the acceptance of their position in Egypt was, however, an act of practical politics. He never attempted to sanction it by the Shari'a. This is the most fundamental difference between his politics and those of Sir Sayyid Ahmad Khan in India. 'Abduh was too good a theologian to permit himself to misrepresent the Qur'an.[13]

'Abduh was more fortunate than his teacher in leaving many works, but he was never able to confine himself to academic tasks. He took a hand in most of the reform movements taking place in the country, be it in the fields of literature, politics, theology, position of women or education. His biographers, taking their line from Rashid Ridha, devote chapters to his activities outside the purely academic pursuits. Adams[14] was certainly justified in devoting a good deal of attention to these activities as manifestations of 'Abduh's basic principles for, despite his writings, 'Abduh's ideas are best approached by the student through both his reform activities and his writings.

The major events in the life of 'Abduh which have influenced his thought fall into two main categories: the personal, that is those events which take place in one's life and decisively affect it but with little if any wider significance; the second category denotes those developments, political, economic and cultural, which engulf one's environment and probably affect the whole world.

Under the first category we may mention the influence of the Sufi Shaikh Darwish who left a profound impression upon 'Abduh's thought and character. Ever since that chance meeting between them and the subsequent interest which the Shaikh took in 'Abduh, Abduh remained for the rest of his life closer to the position of the Sufis than to that of the jurists. Reformism, as we know, is tinged by strong antipathy towards the Sufi orders, but 'Abduh, like his teacher Al-Afghani, gave public support to Sufism in its orthodox manifestations. It was due to his Sufi tendencies that 'Abduh retained a great deal of tolerance and freedom of mind that were unusual amongst his contemporary jurists. When he later joined Al Azhar and became prominent in its affairs, it was natural for him to join with the more liberal Sufi party against the more rigid jurists within the university.[15]

The second such event may have been his meeting with Al-Afghani. It is perhaps difficult to decide whether Al-Afghani, an international phenomenon himself, could be listed under the strictly personal category, but his influence on 'Abduh had the distinct flavour and importance to justify considering it as an event in itself separate from the general impact of Al-Afghani on Egypt or the world of Islam. The relationship between Al-Afghani and 'Abduh appeared to have acquired the character of that of the Shaikh and the Murid in the Sufi order. In his early articles written under Al-Afghani's influence the name of Al-Afghani is always preceded and followed with adjectives that could seldom be found outside Sufi literature.[16] In a particular letter he wrote to Al-Afghani after the former's exile to Beirut, he addresses him in the following terms:

> I wish I knew what to write to you — you know what is in my soul as I know what is in yours, you fashioned me with your hands, and you emanated into my matter its perfect form ... Through you we know ourselves and also through you we know you, and through you we know everything else.[17]

In his preface to this particular letter Rashid Ridha expresses astonishment that 'Abduh should use the language and symbol of pantheism which he always combated; and also at his admission in the body of the letter of his subservience to Al-Afghani, a position that runs contrary to his cherished claim of independence in thought and action. To this writer this letter probably expressed the true nature of the relationship between Al-Afghani and 'Abduh until the collapse of *Al 'Urwat* and the return of 'Abduh to Egypt. 'Abduh's tacit acceptance of the British position in Egypt and his open collaboration with Cromer could not be reconciled with continuous adherence to Al-Afghani's uncompromising antagonism to Britain and his unqualified call for continuous struggle against the invader. Though, as we shall see, 'Abduh described his position as leaving politics to others and concentrating on religious and language reform,[18] his decision to abandon politics was a political act, it is true he did not go as far as Ahmad Khan in India, but to all practical purposes he was of equal value to the British.

'Abduh's emancipation from Al-Afghani's influence began, according to 'Abduh's story, in Paris, where he claimed to have questioned the wisdom of political agitation and preferred concentration on education and writing.[19] This writer suspects that 'Abduh's claim was probably a hindsight. The real difficulty in the relationship between the teacher and the student might have begun when 'Abduh, fearing the consequences in Egypt, sought to hide the fact of his continuing connections with Al-Afghani by refraining from signing a letter to him.[20] The tempestuous Al-Afghani accused him of cowardice, and in consequence the correspondence between the two did not continue. No doubt 'Abduh, finding the gains of collaboration with the British as visible as the possible hardship that would result from antagonising them, thought it wise not to continue his relationship with Al-Afghani. Characteristically, however, he justified his behaviour towards his teacher by a major principle, claiming for himself to have recognised all alone the futility of Al-Afghani's course of action. Such claims must be regarded with scepticism.[21] The ghost of Al-Afghani continued to haunt 'Abduh's behaviour with regard to his famous letter to de Guerville[22] criticising Cromer's educational policy in Egypt, and his conversation with Blunt can only be explained in terms of the conflict between Al-Afghani's militancy and 'Abduh's quiescence.[23]

The major events that shaped 'Abduh's character and thought consisted of those developments which brought aggressive Europe into the heart of Muslim lands and with it its virile culture and technologically oriented civilisation. Like Al-Afghani, he was conscious of Europe as a political force to be resisted and a social ideal to be imitated. In the later years of his life, after he had abandoned the political struggle, his whole effort was devoted to interpreting Islam in terms of modernity. His efforts in this respect, more courageous than successful,[24] brought him fame and a following, particularly amongst the small section of the Muslim population who had been exposed to Western education. In this field, like any other, 'Abduh expanded and deepened Al-Afghani's ideas. In discussing 'Abduh's thought, like those of the major thinkers in modern Islam, it is proposed that four main topics will be discussed, namely: politics, theology, education and legal reform. Though other headings may have claim to be considered, it is my opinion that a clear picture of 'Abduh's position could be obtained from discussing his views on these four issues, and that in consequence it would be possible to predict his position on any other topic. This will be followed by an assessment of 'Abduh as a thinker and of his impact on Egyptian and Muslim thought.

Politics

'Abduh's political thought was a reflection of the circumstances of his environment. In his early days he, like Al-Afghani, concentrated on the politics of Egypt, and for many years after Al-Afghani's departure he continued this interest in his capacity as the editor of the official magazine *Al Waqa'i al Misriyya*. He looked upon the problems of Egypt in terms of national interest transcending religious and racial boundaries. He conceived, again like Al-Afghani, world politics as a struggle between an aggressive West and a victim East. To him this struggle was but a chapter in a long drama in which the two actors, for ever antagonistic, win or lose in accordance with the conditions and implements at their disposal. In an article he published in *Al Ahram* in December 1876 he says, 'This antagonism [between East and West] is hereditary and worthy of consideration but as power has become Western centred and the East has grown defenceless

the West marched in attack and the East could offer no
resistance.' He continued in the vein of Al-Afghani, 'What
made the East reach this low ebb was nothing but disunity to
the extent that some people derive pleasure from having
other Orientals beset with misfortune through enemy conquest.' He then goes on to say

> They do this instead of discarding in these times all reli-
> gious fanaticism and sectarian differences[25] for the
> defence of their homeland and its protection from invasion
> of their enemies. Those enemies wish only to expand their
> domain at our expense, we Orientals, and to be able to
> enslave us so that they may enrich themselves and use us
> as a shield to protect their countries and their men.

And then he significantly declares, 'You Orientals are the
children of one country and the partners in its good and ill
and everything else. If one of you is fortunate, his fortune,
will be a fortune for the others.'[26]

As events developed in Egypt leading to the downfall of
Isma'il and the growth of Anglo-French control and the
expulsion of Al-Afghani, 'Abduh, who was recalled from
his village, where he had been confined by the order of the
Khedive to edit the official journal, found himself in a strong
position to influence events through the use of his pen. His
political articles at this period show two distinct and contradictory trends. Throughout the ministry of Riadh Pasha he
subscribed most faithfully to the cautious, gradual approach
of the Prime Minister. In three articles entitled 'Khata 'Al-
'Ugala', 'The Error of the Wise', he criticised the hotheads
who wished constitutional government to be implemented at
once and he supported the long-term reforms followed by
Riadh Pasha. He continued, however, to speak as a nationalist
who regards the authority of the state to be underlined by
political and geographical boundaries rather than religious
allegiance.

In an article published in November 1881 dealing with
political life, he suggested that the idea of *'watan'* country
is the best unifying factor. He defined it as meaning in the
political sense: 'Your place to which you belong and in which

you have rights and towards which your duties are known and in which you have security for yourself and yours and for your property. He further pointed out that loyalty to the *'watan'* was based on three things. First, that it is the place of residence in which food, shelter, family and children exist; second, that it is the place of rights and duties upon which political life revolves, and third, it is the place to which the person belongs and from which the individual derives glory or shame. This article[27] was published after the fall of Riadh Pasha and its whole tone was to show 'Abduh's conversion to the views of the revolutionaries. In it he declares,

> Some people were attempting to deprive those with duties and rights in Egypt of their nationalist title and to tarnish them with the colour of ignorance and humiliation; but events proved, despite them, that we exist in the national sense and that we have a public opinion.

In December the same year, he wrote about *'Shura'* (consultation) in which he attempted to justify the victory of the 'Urabists in forcing the Khedive to call a national assembly by suggesting that the new system was the modern equivalent of early Islamic tradition.[28] It must be noted, here that whereas Tahtawi in a previous generation suggested that constitutional institutions did not conflict with Islamic tradition, 'Abduh has gone far to claim not merely lack of conflict but complete identity. The consultation or *'Shura'* of the past was to be the consultative assembly of the present. His concept of *'watan'* was borrowed completely from European writers.[29] As there is no such concept in Muslim political thought the whole idea rested uneasily in his thinking. His attempt to relate constitutional advancement to Islam was perhaps motivated by his own need to relate developments to well-founded traditional beliefs whenever possible. The concept of *'watan'* runs counter to the universal community, *'Ummah'*, so basic to Islam. It could only be justified in terms of utility, that is to say as the only possible way for combating enemy threats. The judicial mind could easily accept the necessities of defence, the imperative need to unite the inhabitants of the country and the importance of recruiting non-

Muslim inhabitants of Egypt with their superior skills and ability in the defence against Europe as sufficient reasons for propagating nationalism. Utility and necessity are well established principles of Muslim law but it would defeat 'Abduh's purpose if he were to state that his talk of *'watan'* was only a matter of temporary convenience. His hatred of the Turks reported by Blunt[30] need not have been motivated by patriotism. The idea of a ruling class, race or family, though present in Muslim thought, could not be used to justify Turkish rule. And in any case, the prolonged disappeance of the Quraish and the Arabs in the ruling circle of the Empire has converted many Muslim theologians, chief among them Al-Afghani and 'Abduh, to a near-Khariji position.[31] The secure loyalty which 'Abduh advocated at this stage was therefore dictated by the climate of opinion amongst the many French-educated constitutionalists. However, 'Urabi himself and the whole nation as well as the British regarded developments in Egypt, especially when the British sent their troops against her, as a fight between the Cross and the Crescent. It is important, however, to point out that the betrayal of Egyptian resistance came not from the non-Muslim minorities, but from the Muslim ruling classes and the Muslim Bedouin Arabs.

The occupation of Egypt and the exile of 'Abduh ended for him and his master the nationalist phase of their political thought. In Paris in 1883 they both issued *Al 'Urwat al Wuthqa*, whose positive aim was to unite all Muslims under the Caliphate and to attempt to analyse the factors that led to the decline and fall of Muslims and to charter for them the way to regaining their position.[32] Although *Al 'Urwat al Wuthqa* declares its interest in the defence of Orientals in general and Muslims in particular,[33] the periodical was written in Muslim symbols utilising Muslim beliefs and ideas and drawing for inspiration on Muslim history. It was thus a periodical for Muslims. The catastrophe of Egypt, in its view, was a catastrophe that injured the hearts of Muslims everywhere.[34] *'Watan'* as a bond was now superseded by religion. 'The religious bond between them [the Muslims] is stronger than those of race and language.'[35]

Underlining the editorial of *Al 'Urwat* is an attempt to lay

the theoretical foundations for an *esprit de corps* based on a
new concept of Islam.[36] Though *Al 'Urwat* avoided as much
as possible any direct confrontation with the *ulema*, it nevertheless continued to emphasise Al-Afghani's and 'Abduh's
concept of religion being vindicated in its social manifestations rather than in theological arguments. This *ilhad* (disbe-
lief) was treated as a social disease and an interpretation of
Islam in terms of European culture in the fashion of Sir
Sayyid Ahmad Khan was regarded as treason to the unity of
the *Umma*. Behind the emotional overtone of its articles,
reformism was ushered in. *Al 'Urwat* diagnosed Muslim political failures as resulting from all-too-powerful rulers who are
followed by their nations without question.[37] It was, therefore, logical for *Al 'Urwat* to call upon Muslim nations to
control despotic rulers and effect their removal if it proved
necessary.[38] Like all nationalist ideologies, Muslim nationalism as propagated by *Al 'Urwat* was justified in terms of
history, selectively presented.[39] *Al 'Urwat* also attempted to
activate the lethargy of Muslim communities by arguing
against its theoretical foundation and by minimising the
obstacles and the powers of the enemies.[40]

It is important to note that *Al 'Urwat* attempted to
differentiate between religion and the causes of power. It
regarded Islam as a religion following the same laws as
other religions in its social setting. It also considered that
the laws of nations are applicable also to Muslims whose
Sunni beliefs sought to portray them as the exception to
the rule. The Muslims were therefore told that it is not
enough to be Muslims and they must also partake with
energy and drive in the competition for power and success.[41]
The *Ummah* was addressed in the most flattering terms and
was told that its consensus was sanctioned by God.[42] Its
unity therefore was vital not simply for the defeat of its
enemies but for its very salvation.

After the failure of *Al 'Urwat* and the return of 'Abduh
from exile, he was to disown the idea of unity. Shattered,
defeated and frightened, Muslims had to defend themselves
against accusations of intolerance by intolerant Europe.
While politicians in Britain and elsewhere were conceiving
the struggle openly and expressly as a religious one,[43] the

mere talk of the Muslims' will to defend themselves was labelled fanaticism. To organise and execute actions against Muslims was civilisation. If Europe was ever secular in its political attitudes, the Europe that looked with hatred at the Ottoman Empire on its deathbed was fired by the spirit of the Crusades. 'Abduh, like many other leading figures in occupied Egypt, feared that the spread of Pan-Islamic sentiment and manifestations may bring the wrath of Europe on a defenceless Muslim community.[44] In his biography of Al-Afghani, he attempted to dissociate him from Pan-Islamism. He deliberately confused the aim with the method. That Al-Afghani aimed at Muslim unity is indisputable. In fact his whole career would be meaningless without it. Al-Afghani, however, sought to reach this aim by reforming the political institutions in one country sufficiently to permit the development and progress of such a country which would then become the base for operation. 'Abduh's famous statement suggests that Al-Afghani's

> political aim to which he devoted his thoughts and for which he endeavoured all his life and as a result suffered a great deal was the revival of a Muslim state and guiding it to attend to its affairs so that it might become one of the powerful nations and through her Islam would regain its importance and glory. Implied in this was the humiliation of Britain in Muslim countries and the ejection of its shadow from Muslim communities.[45]

It is obvious even from this statement with its reference to Muslim glory and importance that the final aim of Al-Afghani was Muslim unity, through which alone the glory of Islam would be manifest. In his rejoinder to Hanotaux, 'Abduh rejects Pan-Islamism not on the ground of being invalid but of being impractical.[46] At no time in his career had he conceived Islam without the Caliphate. His return to Egypt, however, with its implied acceptance of British supremacy over Muslims was tolerated by the use of two devices. The first was that politics were outside his main sphere of activities and that political institutions are like trees that take a long time and careful nursing to grow. The second was that

through education and cultural revival the Muslim community would eventually emancipate itself. 'Abduh raised this
into a political creed and paraded this naive concept as a
brilliant political approach to subject Muslims. In Tunisia
and Algeria he counselled the Muslims to avoid political
resistance to France and to concentrate their efforts on
education.[47] The colonial powers gave prominence to the
first part of his advice. The Muslims emphasised the
second.[48] It is doubtful, however, that anyone took 'Abduh
seriously in this respect. At best he was naive, at worst he
was insincere. Very few Muslims thought it possible that
'Abduh would lack the understanding of the true nature of
colonialism. In this connection, Mustafa Kamil following
Al-Afghani points out that colonial powers have the habit
of perpetuating themselves in their position and if a system
of education was seen to lead to their eventual expulsion
they would naturally resist it.[49] As Rashid Ridha pointed
out,[50] 'Abduh's political pacifism was no more successful
with the European powers than Al-Afghani's militance. It,
however, had the disadvantage of taxing the emotions of
Muslims and stretching to breaking point Muslim political
theory in accepting in effect the secularisation of Muslim
politics.

The suspicion that 'Abduh evoked in the minds of his
contemporaries, especially in matters political, may have
prevented him from developing a political theory more in
accordance with the prevailing situation. It was left to the
traditional *ulema* to formulate ideas tacitly accepting non-
Muslim rule.[51] In an essay by Shaikh Muhammad Bakheet,
evidence was purported to have been found for the legitimacy of a non-Muslim Caliph. Strong opposition to the idea
came from Rashid Ridha, who, in the course of his review
of the essay, lamented that whereas the writer could get
away with such an unorthodox idea, 'Abduh would have
run into very serious trouble with the *ulema* had he merely
hinted at it.

'Abduh's withdrawal from politics was simply a withdrawal from nationalist politics. The political intriguer in
him, his deeply set enmity towards the Muhammad Ali
family and the Turkish ruling class brought him into conflict

with Abbas II. The quarrel was motivated, according to
'Abduh, by Abbas' cupidity and 'Abduh's refusal to allow
him to take possession of the Waqf's money.[52] But it is
doubtful that this was the real reason.[53] 'Abduh, like many
who suffered in the aftermath of the 'Urabi revolt, carried
their hatred against the Turkish aristocracy in Egypt to the
extent of supporting the British. Further, the nationalist
movement as epitomised by Mustafa Kamil had at that time
little positive content. The choice offered appeared to be
between the tyranny of Abbas and the autocracy of Cromer.
'Abduh had very little reason to hesitate as to whom he
should choose.

In the age of nationalism triumphant, collaboration with
the enemy is a black mark that must be erased and it must be
explained away in a manner that would make it appear more
like resistance than collaboration. Writing about 'Abduh in
1957, Professor M. Al-Bahay apologises for 'Abduh's relations with Cromer as being a mere measure of convenience
providing 'Abduh with the necessary protection against the
wrath of the Khedive, thus allowing him to continue his
mission of educational and legal reform.[54] As Professor Al-
Bahay has classified 'Abduh as a struggler against Western
expansion, he felt a particular distaste to equating him in his
more genial period with Ahmad Khan of India.[55] Like
Rashid Ridha before him, he fell back on the 'Abduh of the
pre-exile period to provide him with proof of his opposition
to colonialism. In the view of this writer, such an attempt on
the part of Professor Al-Bahay is motivated more by affec-
tion than by hard historical facts. On at least one occasion
Al Manar called for collaboration with the British as the best
possible allies for Islam.[56] No doubt Rashid Ridha then was
reflecting 'Abduh's views.

The attack on Muhammad 'Ali — the ideal Muslim ruler in
the eyes of Al-Afghani — by Muhammad 'Abduh in *Al Manar*
of 1904 was perhaps motivated less by historical analysis
than by his old hatred of that family, antagonism to Abbas,
and sense of guilt at his collaboration with the British. 'Ali
Yusuf, in his obituary of 'Abduh, says that in his later years
he became convinced that he had been God sent to reform
Islam.[57] Such illusions of grandeur emerge in a person of his

intelligence and ability from an insoluble conflict of loyalties, the loyalty to the *Umma* and Islam as he conceived it, and the necessity of collaboration with the British with all its implications.

Like Al-Afghani, 'Abduh opposed autocratic government and subscribed to the idea that a legitimate authority was conditioned by the just application of the law.[58] He believed that rebellion against unjust rulers was legitimate so long as it does not bring greater disasters in its wake.[59] In other words, the potential rebel must weigh carefully his chances of success before embarking on the act of rebellion. He must do so not merely to save his neck but also to save his soul. For it seems as a logical consequence of this view that failure in a noble endeavour is more sinful than not endeavouring at all. Perhaps 'Abduh was not thinking on these lines. He may have had in mind to express the importance of careful weighing of the consequences of rebellion so that legitimate rebellion may not become a licence. Otherwise the whole fabric of political life would disintegrate and anarchy prevail.

The Caliph in 'Abduh's concept was bound by law, deprived of absolute powers, obliged to consult with Muslims, but further he was a civil and not a religious leader. In his reply to criticism of Islam he states that the common criticism of Muslim political institutions among Christians — that Islam supports the identity of religious and political authority — was unfounded.[60] He reasons that the Caliph was simply the political head of the community, he was not its Pope. He did not have the power or the position of the chief priest, nor did he have the exclusive right of interpreting the Will of God. 'Abduh felt, therefore, that Occidentals were unjust to Islam.[61] There is in point of fact a certain justification for 'Abduh's position. Western scholars apply to their studies of Islam principles derived from their own society. The separation between state and Church in the West was simply at least originally a separation between institutions, a definition of functions.[62] It was not intended for the abandonment of Christianity.

The suggestion of separating Islam from politics would be tantamount to abandoning Islam itself, as there is no separate institution equivalent to the Church for the Muslim religion.

To deprive the Muslim community of the support of the political arm of their society to the tenets of their religion is to abolish the religion itself. As we noted earlier, 'Abduh was willing to incorporate Western institutions into the body politic of Islam. In so doing, he opened the way for political development within the Muslim community without the need for heart-searching. Political reform, he contended, is in accordance with the true spirit of Islam. The early Muslims employed institutions suitable to their time and conditions; but Islam as a timeless religion must permit of various forms to fulfil the true aims of its principles.[63]

Theology

'Abduh's fame rests .on his attempt to prove that Islam and modernity are compatible. This position, which he took over from Al-Afghani, was expanded and deepened. The claim, when it was first voiced by Al-Afghani, had two important social functions. On the one hand, it appeased the Western-educated and set their conscience at rest by allowing them to be loyal to both the culture in which they were born and the culture into which they were educated. On the other hand it allayed the fears of the traditionalists who were puzzled by the success of Europe and the failure of Muslims by telling them that Islam could also lead to a similar or even better success than that of Europe. Before Al-Afghani, inasmuch as the *ulema* viewed modernity as incompatible with their religion, they condemned the former and concentrated on the negative side of life subscribing to the most bizarre aspects of decadent Sufism. For this reason both 'Abduh and Al-Afghani voiced strong opposition to prevailing Sufi ideas, just as they did to prevailing legal and theological conceptions.

It is important for us to discern three distinct periods that characterised 'Abduh's thought. Under the influence of Shaikh Darwish and most probably in accordance with his own taste and inclination, his thought was immersed in Sufi ideas. His first work The *Resalat al-Waridat* was an effort in this vein. It was in the tradition of the medieval Sufis. Its ideas, though not departing from acceptable orthodoxy, emphasised those elements that were common in Sufi writing. He later abandoned this position, so much so that in the second edition of Volume II of his biography, Rashid Ridha thought it better not to include *Resalat al-Waridat* amongst his works. In his comments[64] Rashid Ridha says that 'Abduh had changed his position from that of *Al-Waridat* and that it no longer represented his ideas. It must be pointed out, however, that though 'Abduh was writing as a Sufi using the symbols and the language of the Sufis, the ghost of Al-Afghani and his rationalist ideas were not hard to see.[65] Al-Afghani's rationalism, however, drew 'Abduh almost completely out of his Sufi slumber and his next effort was a commentary on the 'Sharhe al Jalal al Diwani ala al Aqa'id Al-Adhudhiyyah'. In this, he showed greater inclination towards philosophy and manifested a liberal attitude towards Muslim disputes.[66] The third stage in 'Abduh's development is what is commonly known as the stage of Salafiyyat.[67] During this stage he drew inspiration from the fundamentalist reform school of Hanbali jurists, in particular Ibn Taimiya and Ibn al-Qayyim and their school. It is this particular stage which Rashid Ridha seeks to advance as the most genuinely representative of 'Abduh's thought. To this phase also belongs his most important contributions, namely the *Resalat Al-Tawhid* and the *Tafsir al-Qur'an* known as *tafsir Al-Manar*.

'Abduh thus travelled from Sufism through rational liberalism to Salafism. It is important to bear in mind that elements of these three trends are always present in his writing.[68] These three stages characterise emphases rather than conversion. This may appear as an oversimplification, but it is important to note that though 'Abduh attempted to revive Muslim philosophy, he had always shown distaste for philosophical encroachment on the domain of religion.[69] 'Abduh consistently showed preference for revelation interpreted by reason, and reason limited in its search for truth by the precepts of revelation. At no time did he rate reason to be above revelation.[70]

Taking the liberal stage in 'Abudh's thought, we note in his non-theological writings a concern for mundane affairs, a preoccupation with the vexed question of East and West, a striving to reach a definite identity for his people as a nation tied together with the bond of patriotism, *wataniyyah*; an identity that tolerates religious differences. That 'Abduh should subscribe to religious and sectarian tolerance is therefore not strange. But what makes sectarian tolerance more significant is that, unlike ordinary nationalists who advocate tolerance because of lack of certainty, 'Abduh suggests that various Muslim sects are equally true and equally acceptable. He quotes with approval the apocryphal tradition which states 'The *Ummah* will be divided into seventy-three divisions all of which will go to heaven except one.' Concerned as he and Al-Afghani were about uniting oriental and particularly Muslim forces in the face of Europe, he tended to minimise theological differences as Al-Afghani attempted before him. But whereas Al-Afghani attributed the extent of the schism between Sunni and Shi'i to the political machinations of rulers, 'Abduh sought to reconcile the various sects through theological manipulation. This phase contributed very little to theological thought as 'Abduh was preoccupied with the political problems of Egypt. His exile concluded this stage of his development and the period of *Al 'Urwat al Wuthqa* may be considered as a period of transition from the liberal attitude to the Salafi trend of thought. Circumstances were the major factor in these developments.

Probably his most important theological work is the *Resalat al Tawhid*. It was originally given as a series of lectures in the Madrassah al Sullaniyyah in Beirut in 1303 Hijra. 'Abduh was then in exile after the failure of the 'Urabi rebellion and the collapse of *Al 'Urwat al Wuthqa*. His other theological works include his reply to Hanotaux and his rejoinder to the onslaught on Islam by Farah Antoun of *Al Jami'ah* magazine, published later under the titles *Al Islam wal Nasraniyyah Ma'a al 'Ilm wa al Madaniyyah* and *Al Islam wa Al-Radd Ala Muntaqidesh (Islam and Christianity in relation to Science and Civilisation* and *Islam and the answer to its critics)* respectively. This last work was by its very nature an apologetic work. Another effort was the articles in *Al 'Urwat al Wuthqa* which predates these two.[71]

The concept of religion emerging from *Al 'Urwat* is one that calls for intense activity, full human participation based on the freedom of will and the concept of moral responsibility. It perceived Islam not simply as a theology but as a civilisation. It is an apologia, for it utilised in the first place its past success and in the second its texts devoid of medieval interpretation. On the other hand it sought in the negative sense to apologise for the failure of Muslims and the success of non-Muslims by linking worldly success to worldly factors, adding however that Islam among religions provides the fittest background for the emergence of the strongest and the most complete civilisation. *Al 'Urwat* therefore accepts the criticism levelled by Westerners, but directs them against Muslim society rather than the faith of Islam. This logic leads to the call that 'the remedy is by returning to the principles of religion, the upholding of its laws as it was in the beginning.'[2]

'Abduh's later writing simply expanded and enriched these ideas. His reply to Hanotaux, for instance, is based on an expanded version of the arguments of *Al 'Urwat*. Hanotaux, who was then a Cabinet Minister in France, wrote an article in the newspaper *Le Journal* dealing with the problem of France's relationship with its Muslim subjects. After a short review of the expansion of Islam and then the growth of European power, Hanotaux pointed out that there were two basic opinions or trends in dealing with Muslims under European rule; one view was extremely antagonistic to Islam, considering it as a disease and calling for the most vicious action against it, including the extermination of one-fifth of the Muslim population and the enslavement of the rest of them in labour camps, and also the destruction of the Ka'aba and the exhibition of the remains of Muhammad in the Louvre. This was contrasted by another which saw in Islam a faith superior to Christianity. In between these two extremes there was another view that regarded Islam as a bridge between paganism and Christianity. The upholders of these last two points of view supported giving aid and assistance to Islam, either as a faith superior to Christianity or as a road to it. That these views were observable aspects of European thought admits no dispute. What brought 'Abduh into conflict with Hanotaux was the latter's assessment or analysis of the causes for the emergence of these views.

Hanotaux thought that though Islam and Christianity shared a common origin in Semitic and Hellenistic cultures, Islam represented more the Semitic mentality with its contempt for man and glorification of the deity; whereas Christianity reflected Aryan humanism that raises man's dignity to that of God. 'The Trinity', says Hanotaux, 'in which man and God unite gives man more dignity, a more central position than the transcendental concepts of Semites which creates a huge gap between an all-powerful God and an all-dependent man.'

This racist concept of culture and religion goes back to Ernest Renan who introduced the idea in *Le Journal de Débats* in 1883. Al-Afghani refuted the concept itself, but it is difficult even in the most learned circles to overcome well-set prejudices, particularly those concerning nations who are visibly weaker. 'Abduh found no difficulty in refuting the theory that the Trinity was superior to transcendentalism. But Hanotaux linked the concept of the Trinity to the idea of free will and Muslim transcendentalism to fatalism and predetermination. It was not difficult for 'Abduh to point out the historical error in this view. Christianity no more than Islam or Judaism solved with any finality the problem of all-knowing God and morally responsible man. Like any other faith, Christianity had its fatalists and it is only due to ignorance that Hanotaux did not see the irrelevance of the Trinity to this problem.

The link between Aryanism and humanism on the one hand and the Semites and monotheism on the other was another historical error that 'Abduh was able to correct. Monotheism, he states was a Hebrew rather than a generally Semitic idea. The Egyptians, the Arabs, the Phoenicians and the Aramaics were all polytheists, following a faith which is nearer to Monsieur Hanotaux's heart than monotheism. Human dignity on the other hand is not impaired in Semitic society. It is so in the Hindu-Aryan religion. 'Would Monsieur Hanotaux', asks 'Abduh, 'consider the caste system, the product of an Aryan race, a manifestation of human dignity?' As regards fatalism and the concept of predetermination, 'Abduh lays the blame for its appearance in Muslim society on the Aryan converts to Islam, especially the Persians and the Romans (meaning Byzantines).

> They [the Persians and the Romans] donned the garb of Islam and carried to it their [older] disputes and hypocrisy. And they introduced the innovation of theological argument and disobeyed Allah and the Prophets who forbade any discussion of Qadar. They deceived the Muslims with their sweet talk and false words until they succeeded in destroying their unity.

'Abduh goes further to suggest that Hanotaux's ranking of religion was wrong. He contended that the higher the civilisation of a community, the greater the intellectual capacity of the individual the closer they become to the belief in a transcendent God. He cites to Hanotaux the rebellion of the great philosophers against Greek mythology, suggesting that Hanotaux seems to venerate the common Athenian at the expense of a Pythagoras, a Socrates, a Plato or an Aristotle. Anthropomorphism was fit for people of low mentality who perceived the world and the things around them in the way they perceive themselves or those who attribute divinity to any extraordinary person. The genius and the hero were divine. There is still a third type who is addicted to anthropomorphism and that is the people who depend on mediators between them and God and who perceive God through the image of their king surrounded by the same entourage and officials through whom one's pleas must go to reach Him. These priests enslave the people and control their thoughts and imagination.

These are the harmful effects of idolatory and its like, which could not be denied.[73] 'Abduh put great emphasis on strict monotheism. Muhammad 'Abduh tells us.

> In its essence true religion is the recognition of a single God who is sole master of the universe. It must consequently be monotheist. It is precisely the case of Islam which has come to call humanity to tawhid, to pure monotheism and to the highest expression of tanzih.[74]

His strict monotheism, however, does not draw him into the arguments pursued by the Mu'tazilites and the Muslim philosophers. He prefers to ignore discussions such as the problem of God's attributes. He says,

> As to whether the attributes are an addition to Him, and
> the attribute of speaking differs from knowledge of the
> contents of revealed books, and that hearing and seeing are
> different from knowing the objects heard and seen, and
> similar problems which divided thinkers and in which
> opinions differed it is not permissible to indulge in, for
> our human reason cannot reach it and the usage of authori-
> tative texts as proof indicates mental weakness and a reli-
> gious deception for as we know language is not confined
> to primary usage. Further language does not bear directly
> on things as they are. These are philosophical ideas which
> if they did not lead the best of them astray have never
> guided any into conviction. We, therefore, must be limited
> to what our reason can handle and to ask God's forgive-
> ness for those who believed in God and in what His
> Messengers brought and who nevertheless indulged in
> discussing these problems.[75]

This last quotation represents the latest stage in 'Abduh's
development, namely his adherence to Salafi principles and
his anxiety to avoid disputes. The technique which he follows
throughout the Resalat is simple. The disputes amongst
thinkers of generations ago were mostly irrelevant or were
caused by a misuse of the language. Irrelevant disputes, such
as the case of God's attributes, were brought in through the
adoption of foreign ideas as the Mu'tazalites did when they
'thought it pious to support religion by the utilisation of
[Greek] science without differentiation between what was
really a fact and with what was only the result of imagination.'[76] 'Abduh goes even further and decries the usage of
philosophy and the application of its methods to theological
problems. To this he attributes the demise of philosophy in
Muslim society.[77] Its sphere he feels should be confined to
those aspects of the physical world that could be useful, such
as the advancement of industry or to improve human organisation.[78] He voices his position unequivocally, 'Our belief
is that Islam is a religion of unity in conviction and not
diversity in principles. Reason is amongst its strongest

supporters and revelation is one of its strongest bases. Beyond this are delusions from Satan and whims of rulers. The Qur'an is a witness on everyone's actions and is the judge of its correctness or error.'[79] This is a far cry from the call of young 'Abduh to study theological and modern sciences which he wrote while still a student of Al Azhar and Al-Afghani.[80] 'Abduh appears to subscribe to the views of his mentors Al-Ghazali and Ibn Taimiya who, though different in their outlook, were one in their extreme opposition to philosophy.[81] 'Abduh found it plausible or perhaps convenient to burden Greek thought with a large share of the dispute amongst Muslims. It was therefore natural that he should seek to ban it as harmful to Islam.

There is of course the added factor that despite its sophistication philosophy did not give any satisfactory answer to the question it undertook to solve. Man, and especially religious man, must fall back on revelation to guide him through the metaphysical maze. Unsatisfactory as this position might appear to the historians of ideas, one must bear in mind that 'Abduh's primary preoccupation was not with providing sophisticated answers to insoluble problems. Rather, he tried to put these problems in what he felt to be their proper perspective. In doing so, he wished to achieve two objectives. The first was to narrow the sphere of doctrinal compulsion, that is to say to limit the number of doctrines to which Muslims must adhere, thus leaving a wide area in which opinion may differ. He, however, advised against wasting effort in attempting to solve the insoluble. The second was to free Islam from a heritage that had become an anachronism. The Perso-Greek element which dominated traditional Islam was incongruous with modernity, and as the emergence of Galilean thought in the West undermined the supreme position of Aristotle, 'Abduh strove to substitute modernity for Greek philosophy.

There was, however, a major difficulty in this procedure. The success which the Muslim philosophers achieved in reaching a compromise between Hellenism and Islam could not be repeated by 'Abduh, as he was both limited in ability[82] and in understanding the true nature of science.[83] The early philosophers appreciated the spirit of Hellenism and were capable of projecting Islam into the universal Hellenistic structure which has previously affected both Christianity and Judaism. They did not perhaps possess precise knowledge as to the contribution of each individual philosopher and this sometimes led to certain difficulties.[84] But what was important was not the ability to pin down the exact ideas of each and every individual. The spirit of Hellenism itself modified by Semitic faith filtered through and was successfully adapted to its new environment by Muslim thinkers. 'Abduh was not so knowledgeable about the West nor was he acquainted to any sufficient degree with science or modern philosophy. His formula was simple: modernity is based on reason, Islam must therefore be shown not to contradict reason, thus we may prove that Islam is compatible with modernity.[85] As a programme this is very limited, and 'Abduh more often than not went beyond this dictum to show agreement between detailed scientific theories or discoveries with Muslim revelation. The Qur'an contains certain things that might not be easily acceptable to the scientifically minded, such as information pertaining to the world of *jinn*, and angels. It even contains apparent astronomical fallacies. 'Abduh would interpret these contents so as to agree with modern discoveries. The *jinns* in this way become the microbes and the story concerning astronomy could be stated to have been addressing simple people at their level of understanding.[86]

Two aspects of modern thought seem to have fascinated him enormously; the one was the theory of evolution which he sought to make compatible with the story of Genesis in the Qur'an and which he employed to prove that Muhammad was the seal of the Prophets.[87] The second is the concept of the scientific law as a formulation of a relationship between cause and effect. 'Abduh was greatly concerned to show that Islam does not reject the principle of causality. He was therefore bent on limiting the region of the miraculous and also on resurrecting the Mu'tazalites' view of the world in preference to the Ash'arite Sunnis who appeared to deny any automatic relationship between cause and effect. For this reason 'Abduh was sceptical of the Karamats,[88] (miracles performed by saints). He used the simple formula of relying on the texts of the Qur'an and the Sunnah without getting deeper into their implications. These ideas could hardly be deemed borrowed from the West. Their origin is firmly oriental and Muslim; yet what forced 'Abduh to make the choice was, among other things, the impact of Western ideas as he understood them.

In his approach to prophecy 'Abduh introduced two new ideas: the first is the evolutionary nature of prophecy referred to above and the second is his emphasis on the moral, social and legal functions of prophets. He lays emphasis on the limits of the prophet's functions. It is not, he makes clear, within their sphere to teach arts or industries or sciences, as the Prophet says: 'You are better acquainted with the matters of industry and artisanship.' This particular idea as we shall see was developed further by his students and by the secularists in their search for a legitimate way of limiting the authority of religion in the life of man.

The emphasis of the social functions of the prophets must bring forth the question of whether they were ever successful. If the prophets and if religion were concerned with making life happier, more successful and more responsible, is it not strange that the Muslims are the least happy, successful and responsible? 'Abduh realises the inevitability of such a question and resorts, as did Al-Afghani, to disclaiming any responsibility on the part of Islam for the failure of Muslims. He continues to attribute success when it occurs in a religious community to its faith and failure to its own action of excess in religiosity or neglect of religion.[89]

'Abduh considers the message of the prophets to be complementary to reason. It cannot possibly contradict it, and it cannot supersede it. 'How', he asks, 'could the place of reason be denied when the proofs of revelation must be sifted and evaluated by it?'[90] But once reason arrives at the conclusion that the claimant to the prophecy is truthful, reason must accept all the information given by him. It must do so even if the nature of some of which are beyond it. In other words revelation can be accepted if it is above reason but not if it is in contradiction with reason.[91] If revelation appears to contradict itself or reason, we must not accept this apparent contradiction, when we have the choice either of interpreting revelation so as to arrive at a consistent meaning or else to spare ourselves the effort and simply rely on Allah. 'Abduh thus resurrects with full force the old principle specifying the relationship between reason and revelation.

His view of religion has certain interesting aspects. He says, for instance, 'Religion is nearer to being an instinctive, intuitive drive than a conscious one. It is one of the most powerful of human forces. It is thus affected in the same way as other human forces.'[92] 'Abduh thus puts Islam on a par with any other faith in so far as it affects human behaviour.

Fundamental to the idea of prophecy in Islam is the doctrine of its conclusion by Muhammad. Theologians have stated that God willed that His communication through revelation with man should end by a specific prophet at a specific time, and that any further claim to prophethood must be regarded as false. The doctrine is supported by numerous verses from the Qur'an and reports of the Tradition. 'Abduh sought to give a sociological rationale to this doctrine. He suggests that revelation varied in accordance with human development, that when man was still in the stage of childhood

It was not wise to address them with high sentiments or reasonable evidence but it would be a sign of mercy to deal with them as a father deals with his young son. He approaches him only through his senses. Thus early religions used powerful commandments and frightening deterrents and demanded complete obedience even in matters beyond their comprehension, though it is clear to us.[93]

The employment of miracles belongs to this stage, in 'Abduh's view, since they aim at overcoming opposition by subduing the emotions. Judaism represents this step in human development. Christianity, on the other hand, is regarded as belonging to a higher stage when perception has gone beyond crude sense perception.[94] It utilised sentiment, emphasised love. Its rituals reflected a tendency to turn away from the world and to Him Most High. It denied man any rights to possess wealth or to demand redress.

The third and highest stage is that of Islam. Here, the world has reached the final stage of development where his own power becomes a major factor in its direction. Hence its message was to be the final one, a religion which addresses man's reason as well as his sentiments and emotions to guide him into happiness in this world and the next. Islam, says 'Abduh, answers all points of dispute proving that the religion of Allah in all generations is one and the same.[95]

The superiority of Islam as a faith does not extend to the fortunes of Muslims in other spheres of life. For generations Muslim scholars, influenced by condemnations of the Jews in the Qur'an,[96] were under the impression that misfortune in this world as well as success resulted from adherence to one particular faith or another. 'Abduh sought to dissociate social and economic conditions from those of religion. In so far as society is concerned, its fortunes are determined by its own behaviour. Individuals do not necessarily suffer the consequences of their misguided actions in this world. The individual pious may suffer misery and unhappiness and poverty in the same way as tyrants and transgressors may enjoy the joys of this world. This, however, is not the case with nations for the law of Allah is unbreakable.[97] It is the Sunnah of Allah that the fortune of people is changed when they themselves change.[98] The spirit which is the basis of progress is contained in all divine religions. No people will suffer so long as they follow this spirit and none will experience happiness, glory, power and comfort without it.[99]

We must therefore accept the claims of the Prophet and believe in his message as contained in the unequivocal texts of the Qur'an and the undisputed Traditions, that is the Tradition transmitted by a sufficient number of people as to exclude the possibility of lying and, on the negative side, we must not add to this belief derived through less certain means.[100] 'Abduh makes it clear that it is essential for Muslims to accept the Qur'an and the practical Sunnah.[101] We must not, however, regard this as an abandonment of the Tradition. 'Abduh was voicing the essentials which constituted Islam and about which there was no dispute. It is, however, another stage to reject the Tradition as a source of Islam. He makes it clear that whoever rejects a thing which he adjudges to have come from the Prophets either through his words or his approval would have rejected the mission of the Prophet and cease to be a Muslim, and similarly with a person who neglects to acquaint himself with the essentials of the faith.[102] He does not bind the Muslim hand and foot by the texts of the Qur'an or the Tradition. In fact he states categorically that so long as the basic beliefs are kept, any interpretation does not exclude the person from being a Muslim. He was aware that many aspects of religion were tailored for the common people rather than the philosophically minded minority, and provided that such a minority upholds the conviction in the existence of Allah, the belief in his Messengers, the hereafter and the respect of the Words of the Prophets, any interpretation of revelation to the satisfaction of their highly developed imagination is not barred. It should, however, not be followed by the common people.[103]

The Moral Law

Among the questions that stirred earlier Muslims was the one of the moral law, namely whether actions in themselves can be adjudged virtuous or evil and whether human reason is capable of discovering this unaided. This problem appeared in Mu'tazalite thinking as a consequence of their concept of the deity. Having conceived of God as the source of good they limited His actions to what accords to His nature. They also felt that evil to be punishable must be caused by man. To the Sunnis this view appeared closer to the old Persian belief in two forces, one for good and one for evil. The spirit of Islam, they believed, attributes everything to the creator. Goodness and badness in an action are relative aspects and could not be applicable to Allah. To punish the pious and reward the sinner is unjust only in our minds. Who are we to judge the owner of everything and the creator of everything? A judgement of this nature subjects Allah to the law of man. This Sunni view means in effect that the moral law is not an objective one, nor could it be arrived at through the pursuit of human reason alone. What is good is what Allah informs us through the prophets is good. Similarly, what is bad is what Allah names bad. Reason must accept the dictates of revelation. To the Mu'tazalites such an argument would end up by making man no different from a feather in the wind, thus destroying the very basis of moral and religious responsibility. Punishment and reward as promised by Allah necessitate freedom of action on the part of man and an inherent value in his actions. Implied in this is man's ability to discover for himself these values. Revelation would simply confirm what reason has already arrived at. The concept of God is thus at the heart of the argument. Is He the absolute and unquestioned ruler or is He some sort of constitutional monarch who like his subjects must adhere to the law?[104]

In his attempt to solve the problem of the moral law, 'Abduh, following earlier Muslim scholars,[105] treated it as part of the general question of value.[106] Thus he uses the term beautiful to mean also good, and ugly denoting also evil. This procedure makes it possible to start from the concrete and move up to the abstract, so 'Abduh begins with the beautiful, stating that, 'We find in ourselves the ability to distinguish between the beautiful and the ugly.'[107] He observes that this applies to all sense modalities and that without having to go into the definition of beauty and ugliness it is not 'a subject of dispute, that it is a characteristic of man and some animals to distinguish between the two.'[108] He therefore concludes that 'things in themselves have beauty and ugliness.'[109]

Abstract ideas have also beauty and ugliness, though not as easily perceptible as with concrete objects. It is in his view connected with perfection and the lack of it, so the 'perfection of the abstract such as the absolute and the spirit and the human qualities has a beauty which the souls of those who know it feel.'[110] In contrast, lack of perfection has ugliness which can similarly be perceived. No one can dispute the ugliness of a lack of intellectual ability and similar shortcomings. That is why those who suffer from these shortcomings exert their utmost to hide them.

'Abduh concedes that sensory judgement can be modified by experience; thus things which may appear at first encounter ugly could become beautiful through their consequences or their association with what is beautiful. Thus a bitter medicine may be judged on the basis of its curative potency;

just as a sweet food may be judged in accordance with its harmful consequence. From things 'Abduh moves to actions and feels that they share existence with things and therefore should share the same classification into beautiful and ugly. He has three categories of actions:

1. Actions beautiful in themselves like military parades, gymnastics or music; or ugly in themselves like the movements of the mob in a crisis and the sound of the lamentation of women;

2. Actions judged according to their consequences so every action which might cause pleasure or ward off pain is beautiful, while the opposite is ugly.

These two categories 'Abduh finds common to man and higher mammals. The difference between them is only a matter of degree.

3. The actions which have to be judged on their delayed consequences. In other words, the actions which will have to be considered not on the crude hedonic principle but on the principle of utility. Thus actions are beautiful if they are useful and ugly if they are harmful. This category is characteristic of man.[111]

'Abduh considers this to be axiomatic. He, following the Muslim philosophers, believes that man would arrive through the use of his reason to whether an action is moral or immoral. Since this depends on a quality in the actions in themselves, he brands those who oppose this view as depriving themselves of their reason.[112] He suggests that an ethical system based on reason alone is possible although it is not within the capacity of the common people to discover it.[113]

He sees moral judgement to be influenced by man's memory, imagination and thinking. Since individual differences are only too evident with regard to these faculties differences as regards the specific judgement on actions as moral or immoral correspondingly differs. Therefore human reason alone cannot achieve happiness in this world except with regard to a few individuals. Hence the need for guidance and this guidance is provided by the Prophet.

Through this psychological analysis 'Abduh was able to give strong support to the Mu'tazalite point of view[114] and, through his sociological observations of the endless differences as to what is good and what is bad, he approaches the position of the Ash'arites. The idea that the élite can arrive at the highest religious and ethical concepts is acceptable to most schools of Muslim thought.

Education

Al-Afghani's school set great store on education. In numerous places Al-Urwat emphasises the important role of education and as referred to above the *Ulema*, whose most important function is teaching, occupied a pivotal place in Al-Afghani's scheme of things. Like him, 'Abduh pinned his hopes for the survival of Islam and progress of the community on the improvement of its education. As is the nature with 'Abduh's life, three distinct periods can be distinguished, each representing a dominant view in education: his pre-exile period ending in 1882, his activities during his exile which ended with his return in 1889, and the period after his return until his death.

In his early days under the influence of Al-Afghani, he recognised most clearly the shortcomings of Al Azhar education. In an article written in 1877,[115] he called for the introduction of modern sciences together with the local sciences into Al Azhar university, and describes the strength of prejudice against them in Al Azhar and popular circles. He related the story, which was almost certainly his, of a student who ran into trouble with his father on account of indulging in these disciplines and how he had to swear that he would waste no time on them. He decried Al Azhar's failure to study these disciplines, some of which were being read in most Muslim mosques, even in the capital of the Caliph himself. He relates that Al-Ghazali and others considered the study of logic and similar disciplines obligatory for the defence of Islam, and he felt that 'In these days where peoples of many religions meet, it is clear that what our forefathers handed down and what our relatives informed us if not supported by evidence will be attacked by heretics and unbelievers.'[116] He goes on to say:

> If this is our position in relation to disciplines which grew in Muslim environments for the last thousand years and which were inherited by us, what I wonder will be our position in relation to the new and useful sciences which are essential to our life in this age and which is our defence against aggression and humiliation and which is further the basis of our happiness, wealth and strength. These sciences we must acquire and we must strive towards their mastery.[117]

He argues the case for modern sciences in the classical legal fashion. He says.

> There is no religion without a state and no state without authority and no authority without strength and no strength without wealth. The state does not possess trade or industry. Its wealth is the wealth of the people and the people's wealth is not possible without the spread of these sciences amongst them so that they may know the ways for acquiring wealth.[118]

In the vein of Al-Afghani he calls upon the *Ulema* to advise the people on this score and he apologises for them not having done so previously by claiming that

> They did not pay attention to its necessity . . . Had they paid such attention and scrutinised the matter as it is, they would have worked hard to guide the people in this direction and they would have filled the mosques with speakers and preachers to urge the public to acquire what is essential for the protection of their faith.[119]

These were the sparks of an enthusiastic young student who felt strongly about his belief and who was aware from first-hand experience of the tremendous opposition and difficulty. Later, as an editor of the official journal *Al-Waqai' Al-Misriyyah*, he concerned himself with education and campaigned against educational policy during the 1880s to the extent that the then Minister of Education complained to the Prime Minister who in his turn stood by 'Abduh. He requested the Minister to take 'Abduh's criticisms seriously, and to assist him, and in this respect an educational committee with 'Abduh as a member was instituted. Although the majority of members were Europeans, 'Abduh managed to obtain approval for the proposal that the Ministry be given the right to supervise foreign schools in the country. The question of the schools was important as they were regarded by Muslim opinion as less educational in nature and more as religious propaganda centres. 'Abduh's success in this direction was, however, nullified by the coming of the British.[120]

'Abduh was aware of the importance of education in matters of cultural influences and was critical of parents who allowed their children to be educated in missionary schools. In a somewhat amusing incident he and Al-Afghani once waded through the muddy streets of Alexandria for the sole purpose of re-converting a Muslim youth who under the influence of the missionaries in his school had become Christian.[121] Both were disturbed at the lack of concern in this respect of authorities in Egypt. 'Abduh expressed his view on foreign schools in no uncertain terms in an article published in August 1881 dealing with the influence of education in matters of religion and faith. He points out the obvious fact that

> The missionary schools were not established for the purpose of profit but for the sole object of spreading knowledge and lighting the candle of civilisation, or so they say, such as the Frere schools of American and English origin and others. Assuming that we accept what they say regarding their intentions in establishing these schools, it is a fact that the heads of these schools belong to one sect of Christianity or another. Headmasters are not obliged to issue special religious books to each student in accordance with his particular religion . . . and do not feel it their duty to employ religious teachers of a different denomination. They naturally specify religious books in accordance with their own outlook. This is the

reason that all books in these schools fit in with the religious and sectarian beliefs of the headmaster. The Protestants use Protestant books, and the Catholics use Catholic books and so on and so forth. The students despite their religious differences are made to read one and the same type of book which accords with the particular beliefs of the founder of the school. If the students are exposed for a long time to the education in a Protestant school, for instance, there is no doubt that their beliefs will gradually change from the Coptic, Catholic or Islamic faith to the Protestant religion. This is also true in the case of the Catholic schools or the Muslim Maktabs such as the Qur'anic maktabs or the school of Al Azhar.[122]

He consequently calls upon parents to refrain from sending their young children to schools established for the propagation of a different denomination or religion.

Muslim revivalism owes a great deal to the activities of the missionaries, which for the most part were crude, arrogant and ignorant. This caused Muslims to resent them and suspect everything European.[123] As European influence grew in Egypt, so did the arrogance and irresponsibility of the missionaries. The fate of most missionary establishments in Egypt in the era of colonial withdrawal need not stimulate any pity or sorrow. The historical process necessitates the destruction of an educational system which was regarded as having derived its existence, its *raison d'être* from European military superiority and from the desire to soften local resistance to European supremacy respectively.

'Abduh's opposition to the missionaries was in no way an opposition to Western science and technology. The essence of his reform is to introduce them into Muslim life. He was, however, opposed to imitation of Western institutions without any reference to the cultural milieu of the Muslims. Like Al-Afghani, he distrusted the Westernisers and he lumped them together with the conservatives under the derogatory nomenclature of Muqallidun (imitators).

The Westernisers in Egypt were adopting Western education, Western sciences and even a Western medium of teaching, namely French. 'Abduh, in a strong article in *Al-Waqai'*,

December 1880, strongly criticised the decision of the Ministry to use a foreign medium even in a school meant for popular education. He reminds his readers that 'Evening schools in civilised countries teach sciences through the medium of the colloquial language, refraining as much as possible from the use of technical terms which might be difficult to understand.' He then sarcastically asks 'Is it possible that we have become more advanced than these civilised countries and that our evening schools have become of a higher level than theirs?' He draws attention to the fact that the student population in these schools consisted largely of foreigners and points out that the language of primary education, particularly in the evening schools, must be the language of the country; thus the ignorant and the lazy would have no excuse in not joining them.

'Abduh comments with scorn on a directive by the Ministry of Education threatening punishment for various shortcomings in the teaching profession. He reminds the Ministry that 'Decrees and high pronouncements without something tangible coming out of them have no place.'[124] He calls upon the Ministry to see that simplified books in the Arabic language are written and made available to the students.[125]

In the opinion of 'Abduh the purpose of education is 'To bring up minds and souls and to raise them to the point where the person becomes capable of achieving full happiness or as much of it as possible in his life and after death.' 'Abduh rejects the mechanical view of schools and educational institutions as merely factories producing skilled robots. His view is that the school and the whole system of education must help a person mentally and spiritually:

> We mean by the education of the mind bringing it out of simplicity and emptiness of knowledge and away from false concepts and bad ideas so that it acquires correct concepts and information. From this the mind becomes capable of distinguishing between good and bad, harmful and useful. This must reach the point of becoming a *SAJYYAH* [second nature].

This he regards as the first pillar of education. The second, however, is to do with the spirit.

> We mean by the education of the souls the creation of
> qualities and good manners in the soul and training her in
> them and keeping her away from bad qualities so that the
> person grows up in accordance with the rules of human
> society and accustomed to them.[126]

'Abduh recognises that the two pillars are essential for
education to have any significance or use. To him this fact
is axiomatic. 'Abduh, it must be realised, was not a friend of
free thought. He might have chided his opponents as imitators either of the classical writers or of Western ideas, but he
did not for that reason give free rein to the individual to find
his own way. When appointed as the editor of the official
magazine he became the *ex officio* censor of literature and
books. He advocated a stern supervision of what the people
were allowed to read. Once more he took himself to be the
measure of all things. He used this authority to prevent
the circulation of books which he considered to be corrupting or a waste of time. It is, however, significant that while
objecting to the traditional epics of Egyptian society he
commended certain French novels that were serialised in
the Egyptian press of the time.[127] In another context he
chides those advocating freedom in personal behaviour,
pointing out that the consequence of their so-called freedom
of opinion was the destruction of religion and the release of
the basest desires. This so-called freedom was not, he
observed, based on any consistency of ideas for 'I have met a
person who though denying that God existed went on to ask
about the significance of Muhammad's ascension to heaven,
while others deny prophecy and at the same time believe
in Satan and things of this nature.'[128]
    'Abduh's authoritarian vein runs through his ideas whether
political, educational or religious. The freedom of the mind,
as he advocated it, was one of a very limited nature, as his
attitude to the public was one of strong paternalistic
flavour.[129] After his exile from Egypt his interests in education became concentrated on religious education. Like Al-
Afghani he saw a nefarious conspiracy behind any movement

of Westernisation in the Muslim world. He subscribed to Al-Afghani's views of Ahmad Khan and his ideas, especially his advocacy of co-operation with the British. In *Al-'Urwat*, Ahmad Khan was branded as a British agent to ruin Muslim beliefs and weaken their zeal for their religion.[130] Inasmuch as *Al-'Urwat* concerned itself with the problem of education which was only by the way and incidental to its main concern, namely politics, it advocated a rise of the *Ulema* to their duty of informing the public as to the principles of their religion and creating a climate under which the Muslims can in unity acquire knowledge of science and technology to match and even beat Europe. At the same time, Muslims were expected to live up to the ethical principles of their religion which, in a sense, meant a greater social conscience.[131] Naturally *Al-'Urwat* was concerned with education only in the most general sense, that of influencing public opinion towards a particular direction, namely Muslim unity and resistance to Western aggression. Al-Afghani, however, had certain ideas about education and he voiced them in this fashion:

Educational disciplines are aimed at the preservation of the virtues of the soul and remedying them if the soul falls short or goes astray, in the same way as medicine is aimed at the preservation of bodily health. The practical sages who concern themselves with education and guidance and the clarification of the distinction between bad and good and the transformation of the souls from imperfection to perfection are in this way similar to the physicians.[132]

After the collapse of *Al-'Urwat* and 'Abduh's return to Beirut and the invitation to teach in Al Madrassah Al Sultaniyyah, 'Abduh became more and more concerned with education in the specific sense. In a speech he gave to the school he states that

The science which we feel in need of is thought of by some people to be technology and other means of mastering agriculture and trade. This is false, for if we look at what we complain of, we find something deeper than the mere lack of technology and similar disciplines. If technology was mastered by us we would find ourselves unable to keep it on. Though opportunities for benefiting ourselves come our way, they soon go and that is because of something within ourselves. We complain of lack of ambition, laziness, disunity, disregard of obvious interest. Technology cannot offer us remedies to such complaints. What we need to learn, therefore, is something beyond such a discipline, that is the discipline which touches upon the soul and this is the science of human life . . .[133]

In his view,

The science which will revive the souls is the science of disciplining the soul. Such a discipline exists only in religion, therefore what we lack is extensive knowledge of the ethics of religion and what we need in accordance with our feelings is to have a true understanding of religion.[134]

During his stay in Syria he submitted two proposals for the reform of religious education. The first was for the Shaikh Al Islam in Istanbul and the second was to the Governor of Beirut. His suggestion was that the improvement in education would be a protection for the Caliphate. He shuns nationalism, public interest 'and similar high sounding words' in favour of religion as a motive force for stimulating Muslims towards the desired aim. He describes Muslims as having suffered from ignorance to the point that they are indistinguishable from animals. This he felt was because of religious weakness which he suggested 'opened the door to the foreign devils to reach the hearts of many Muslims and to sway them to fall in with their conspiracies and to listen to their tempting words'.[135] He observes that there is no place in the Muslim world without a school for the Americans, Jesuits, the Freres and other religious organisations. He mourns the fact that Muslims no longer objected to sending their children to these schools because their graduates have a better chance of earning a living, either because of their education or their knowledge of a foreign language. He warns that these schools are a danger to Islam and to the whole concept of Osmanism. He deals with the Muslim Maktabs and Madrassahs and points out that whatever religious education is claimed to exist there, it is far too inadequate and too formalistic to have any effect on the character of the Muslim student. He links the general distaste for military service to this ignorance of religion and weakness in conviction.

For his proposal he divides his Muslims into three groups or classes: the first is the general public, consisting of the artisan, tradesman and agricultural people, the second is the government servants, whether civil or military or judicial, and the third is the *Ulema* class whose concern is the guidance and education of the people. He stresses that these divisions are not meant to be permanent. Anyone who acquires the necessary qualifications can be admitted to the higher class.[136]

His specific educational programme for the general public would be the three Rs and a simple book on Muslim theology containing all the agreed principles among the Sunnis 'refraining from any reference to disputes between Muslim sects and supporting them with easily understood proofs . . . verses of the Qur'an and authentic Traditions should be used in evidence.' It is clear that he aimed at reducing the differences as much as possible between Muslims, an aim which has influenced his action and thought throughout his life. To emphasise this he suggests that such a general book should contain some references 'to the disputes between us and the Christians and making clear the faults of their beliefs so that their [students'] minds would be ready to defend Islam against the allegations of Christian missionaries.'[137] For the inspiration of the public he advises the teaching of a brief account of the Sirah and the history of early Islam and the days of Muslim glory followed by a brief history of the Osmani Caliphs.

'Abduh, like Al-Afghani, was well aware of the role of history as an instrument of public policy. Nothing can give a nation an inspiration more than a reference to a past glory, real or imagined. Modern nationalism relies on a great many myths of past achievements. Muslim history, however, can, if selectively presented, offer such an inspiration and 'Abduh was simply advising such a course.

For the second class he offers similar but more intensive courses. The study of history at this stage must emphasise the purely religious side and it must be calculated to incite Muslims to regain the lost lands of Islam.

The third class, unlike the first two, must learn in Arabic and must read an intensive course in the various Muslim disciplines. It is noticeable that again he suggests that the study of history must be aimed at proving that the cause of Muslim contemporary difficulties was only religious ignorance.

He makes it clear that the aim of his programme is to establish the position of religion so deep in the heart of the students that it directs their every action, thus uniting them materially and spiritually in the service of Islam and 'the support of the great protector of Islam and the defender of its land, the Amir al Mu'minin'.[138]

'Abduh appears to use the same technique of persuasion, namely identifying the aims of his programme with those of the powers-that-be at whatever time and place they happen to be. 'Abduh calls further for the training of a number of this last class to become preachers. This particular idea he claimed to have had in his mind for a long time. It may have inspired his student, Rashid Ridha, into establishing a school for preachers. His memorandum to the Governor of Beirut is more a report on the actual situation of the Muslims in the area than a programme. He points out the fact that the Muslim Sunni is the citizen upon whom the Ottoman state must rely and whose education must thus be its primary concern, to make him into an effective instrument. Other groups such as the Christians, the Druze, the Shi'ites, the Nusayriyyah have for one reason or another felt disenchanted with Ottoman power. Behind this disenchantment there is always a foreign agent utilising missionary techniques to create dissension. He thus invites the Governor to introduce proper education for these various groups to ensure their loyalty.

'Abduh returned to Egypt in 1889 greatly mellowed and resigned to live with an Egypt ruled by the British. Characteristically, he sought a position of power, namely a teaching post or even the principalship of Dar-Al-Ulum. Without many qualms or hesitation he sent a note to Cromer containing his views on education and putting suggestions to show that his views accorded with the aims of Cromer in Egypt, especially in reaching a position where Egyptian Muslims would feel no religious objection to British rule. He points out that because of political rivalry amongst European powers the incitement of Egyptians to rebel against the British was ceaseless, and he points out that religion has the greatest influence on the minds of Egyptian Muslims, and those bent on creating dissension in the country need only say that the ruler of your country 'is not of your religion and you are enjoined to hate him and to use every opportunity to overthrow his power'.[139]

To ensure Egyptian co-operation and compliance, he suggests a system of education taking its basis from Islam. There is no reason to suspect that Islam by its very nature need stand in the way of co-operation between Muslims and non-Muslims. 'The true religion of Islam is not against friendship and it does not war against love, nor does it forbid Muslims taking advantage of the actions of those of other religions with whom they have common interests.'[140] He points out that only through religion could any system of education succeed in Egypt. Purely secular education must fail.

> The best evidence on the failure of the system of education which is called literary education [meaning secular] is the effect of such a system from the time of Muhammad 'Ali to this day. Its products became worse despite their greater knowledge but since their general knowledge and demeanour were not based on the principles of their religion it left no effect on their souls.[141]

'Abduh's criticism of secular education was undoubtedly sound. It has brought great hardship and dislocation to those exposed to it without safeguards. The duality of education systems in Muslim countries was the direct result of this concept of secularisation. Its consequences, social and educational, were so damaging that now it has become the trend throughout the emergent countries to merge the two streams into one, that is to create an honourable and meaningful place for the native culture in the largely Western system. 'Abduh was certainly aware of the harmful effects of educational dualism. In his letter to Cromer, 'Abduh suggested the unification of education in Egypt through the development of Dar-Al-Ulum so that it could in future replace Al Azhar.[142] He observes that education under Muhammad 'Ali had failed to achieve much in the way of training or character-building. Muhammad 'Ali's aim, 'Abduh asserts, was not true education but simply the training of some children in disciplines such as engineering, medicine and translation so that they would be able to fill the necessary posts in the system of government which he created. 'As for education based on sound ethical grounds, it has never occurred to him nor to those who run his schools.'[143]

After a gap of neglect between Muhammad 'Ali and Isma'il schools flourished again; but Isma'il's aim was simply to give Egypt a Westernised veneer so that 'it might be said that he has in his government something similar to that of European governments.'[144]

Foreign schools being representative of a different culture were seen by 'Abduh as more harmful than useful. The conflict between such a school and the Muslim home was inevitable, as it was necessarily confusing for the child. 'Abduh touches on a sensitive nerve by reminding Cromer that these schools

> caused Muslims to shy away from the heads of these schools and the nations from which they originated. Their history in this country is well known. They are harmful to friendship, against good relations despite the claims of those who run them. As a system of education it cannot supplant the national schools in its different forms.[145]

He describes the state of Al Azhar, its spiritual and educational degeneration, and calls for urgent though gradual reform. He points out that there is no need to fear the antagonism of its *Ulema* as Isma'il did when he attempted to introduce technical education. He assures Cromer:

The situation has transformed and reform has become easier in Al Azhar than in any other public institution in Egypt. Any Chief Minister can effect such reform almost effortlessly, and whatever the Chief Minister feels unable to do, the writer of this document undertakes to effect if charged to do so.[146]

He, however, makes one point very clear, that the reform of Al Azhar depends on the reform of the government school system. If this reform is effected, no one, 'Abduh felt sure, would choose Al Azhar and the unification of the education system becomes a reality. In his reference to the primary government Maktabs, 'Abduh suggests, among other things, that the history of Egypt should be studied with reference to 'what the country has suffered in the past and the comfort which it has now reached'.[147] He further suggests the teaching of civic duties so that the 'student may learn to submit and follow every official in whatever directive might come from him'.[148]

In his reference to the preparatory and higher education institutes he points out that education in its proper sense does not exist in them, and suggests the introduction of religious and moral education to ensure that the graduates, if not employed by the government, will find other work without becoming disenchanted with the régime. His final comment is even more revealing. He seeks to tempt Cromer to his views by reminding him that education is the instrument of the government in directing its subjects and in pointing out that his suggestions would be more beneficial than Ahmad Khan's in India and would not stimulate such suspicion as Khan's did. In the last paragraph he says,

I repeat that whoever sows will reap the best fruit and the value of this project will go beyond, into other, countries and will be beneficial to the originator. In a short while its success will be evident to the person in power [meaning Cromer] and to those ruled by him. He will be able to decide on those who have benefited by this reform in the spirit of friendship and understanding and not on the basis of fear and terror. In this way he would have created for

himself a new people to help him in the hour of need and
support him in times of trouble and back him in any difficulty. It will erase from the minds of the people any
attachment to others. Obstacles created by blind *[jahili]*,
fanaticism will disappear from his way together with
unwise fanaticism dressed up as concern about religion.
In my view opposition to this project constitutes an opposition to his power.[149]

As a final exposition of 'Abduh's educational ideas we may
profitably refer to his practical application of these theories.
'Abduh, after a long interval, was able (probably with the
help of Cromer) to persuade the Khedive of the need of
reform in Al Azhar. A committee was therefore formed with
'Abduh as a member. He was firmly convinced that the
reform of Al Azhar would be of great benefit to Islam. The
conservatism of its *Ulema* was recognised by 'Abduh as the
greatest obstacle. His enthusiasm for reform and hope for a
speedy transformation appeared to have been dampened by
the advice of others. Rashid Ridha reports him as saying, 'If
the conditions of Al Azhar are improved before I die I shall
go full of happiness. Indeed I shall feel like a king.'[150] He saw
the problem of Al Azhar in simple terms; either it should
reform or it should completely collapse. And though he very
often linked the destiny of Islam with that of Al Azhar, he
thought that the disappearance of Al Azhar need not cause
despair for Islamic reform. He appeared at this stage to have
convinced himself that he had joined the government solely
for the purpose of reforming Al Azhar. It was therefore
natural that he should say to Rashid Ridha again that if
reform proved impossible in Al Azhar,

I shall resign my government post and choose a number of
suitable persons and educate them in the Sufi method as
I have been so that they may succeed me in the service of
Islam. Then I shall write a book to expose Al Azhar, the
ethics of its people, their mental capacity and the degree
of their knowledge together with their influence. I shall
then publish the book in Arabic and a European language
so that Muslims and non-Muslims will become aware of the

true nature of this place.[151]

One must note in this outburst elements of frustration lead-
ing to an exaggeration of his own position and abilities.
Were the behavioural manifestations of this feeling respon-
sible (at least partly) for what 'Ali Yusuf referred to as
'Abduh's thinking of himself as the God-sent reformer of
Islam?

The activities of the Committee of Al Azhar were recorded
in a booklet written by 'Abduh's friend and collaborator,
Abd Al-Karim Salman, who was also a member of the
Committee.[152] The efforts of the Committee were frustrated
by outside factors. It was probably a misfortune that the
reform of Al Azhar was so cleverly identified with 'Abduh,
who was prominent in the Cromer party. Al Azhar therefore
became one of the areas of conflict between the Khedive and
Cromer. 'Abduh became a central figure in this dispute. Since
any success in reforming Al Azhar at that time would have
been a victory for 'Abduh (and Cromer), the policy of the
Khedive (and the nationalists) was directed at supporting the
conservative wing of the *Ulema*. 'Abduh in his turn was too
ambitious to solve the problem by withdrawing from the
scene and thus allowing the advancement of his policies but
not his person to take place. A number of administrative
reforms were adopted, but what was much more important,
the academic reform, was almost totally rejected. Even so,
it would be erroneous to think that the majority of the
Ulema were not well aware of the value of academic reform
or that they believed that modern sciences 'wreck the basis
of religion and corrupt the conviction of the Muslims'.[153] As
Rashid Ridha observed, many of them sent their children to
be educated in the modern disciplines in government schools.

In the face of the strong conservative opposition to
reform, Cromer was content to stand neutral. He prevented
the Khedive from dismissing 'Abduh, and thus from gaining a
full victory.[154] But he would not support 'Abduh in any
positive way to reform Al Azhar, probably because he
thought that the case for Islam in the modern world was a
hopeless one.[155]

'Abduh always regarded himself as a teacher. His concern

with education was therefore closer to his heart than any other cause. He appeared to have read some Western works on education and he translated from the French Spencer's Essay on Education.[156] There is, however, little echo of these ideas in 'Abduh's programme, probably because 'Abduh learned French late in life and also the situation he faced within Al Azhar demanded immediate practical reform at a level that hardly necessitated any deep theoretical formulations.

'Abduh wished to end the duality of education and ensure the relevance of the school to the home and cultural environment. His aims in this respect would have the complete support of modern educationalists.

Legal Reform

Islam is the religion of the law. Any reform must by necessity use the law as its instrument and most obvious manifestation. The school of Al-Afghani attacked first and foremost the authority of those writers in the era of decadence whose books were studied throughout the Muslim world as the final arbiters in matters of law. True, jurists have always allowed for necessary social change to be accommodated within the system, thus reducing the tension between the ideal and the actual. The history of Islam in its legal aspect is a story of adjustment between the decrees of God and the needs of man. The impact of modernity, however, imposed such a radical transformation in Muslim society that piecemeal adjustment was no longer adequate.[157] The *Ulema* whom Al-Afghani reported as declaring Islam to be incompatible with modern science were in fact stating the true assessment of the situation.[158] Traditional Islam, as it was then, had no place for modernity. The school of Al-Afghani never disputed this assessment. It simply attempted to introduce a new Islam unsaddled by medieval thought, thus allowing for greater accommodation with modernity. 'Let us go back to the Qur'an and the authentic Tradition' was the cry of every movement for change in Islam. The school of Al-Afghani, however, gave it a new twist. It claimed not only that Islam was compatible with modernity but that it creates the best environment for modern civilisation.

Egypt, under the impact of Europe, adopted a number of institutions, political, economic and educational, which were unknown in the Middle Ages when the books of law were written. They were introduced so rapidly and, under Muhammed 'Ali, without any consultation with religious authorities,[159] that they became an accepted feature of Egyptian life. Al-Afghani sought to bridge the gap between a system of law and an actuality that it no longer reflected. His device was simply to reject *Taqlid* (blind imitation) and to advocate *Ijtihad* (independent thinking) in matters of law. He was well aware of the function of (*Ijma'*) the general consensus of the *Ulema*, the leaders of the community or the community as a whole as a Muslim device to legitimise change.[160] But Al-Afghani and his school did not want to be hampered by an *Ijma'* that in their view was useless, even dangerous.[161]

The new institutions in Egypt were on the whole transplanted into the community and did not spring from it. The fact that the *Ulema* did not feel any urgency for the legitimisation of these institutions is an indication of how far they represented an emotional problem to the Muslims of the day. To the *Ulema* the whole issue of modernisation became an insoluble problem. This was perhaps one of the reasons that Al-Afghani and his students were suspected as enemies of Islam seeking to violate its precepts for the benefit of non-Muslims. Since Al-Afghani did not offer any specific programme beyond the call for a new *Ijtihad*, and since he later consumed his energy in the service of Muslim political unity, his name was hardly tarnished on this score. It fell to 'Abduh and, later, Rashid Ridha to put more definite solutions to the problems of the day.

Europe at that time was in the grip of a bourgeois revolution and to 'Abduh, Islam was to be interpreted in a way to effect the greatest congruity with bourgeois ideas. There is, however, a certain degree of restraint that must be exercised by the Muslim jurist, for on the one hand the Qur'an must be accepted as the absolute and final authority in matters legal, on the other the schools of law with their established institutions could not be dismissed out of hand. 'Abduh's legal reform, however, consisted primarily of resurrecting an old principle and giving it respectability. This principle was in effect what the Muslim jurists used to call *Talfiq*, that is following more than one school of thought in the performance of one or more actions. As the differences between schools sharpened, it bordered on the heretical to deviate from one's own school to any other. 'Abduh, realising the great advantage in flexibility which would accrue through the adoption of the more liberal policy, suggested the use of all schools of thought and the works of all the *Ulema* as a source from which to select the most suitable legislation for any current problem. In essence, therefore, what 'Abduh was calling for was the abandonment of specific Taqlid in favour of a general one. Throughout his career he never deviated from the established schools of law.[162] Sometimes he addressed questions sent to him on a point of law to the leaders of the various schools of law in Al Azhar to ascertain their opinions before issuing his own.[163] The controversies that some of his judgements cause arose from his own personal position and his political role and rarely from a purely legal dispute.[164] His judgement in the Transvaal Fatwa was attested to by even the most conservative amongst the *Ulema*. He could count amongst his supporters many jurists with traditional inclinations, such as the leader of the conservative faction in Morocco, who, however, attacked 'Abduh for doctrinal rather than legal opinion.[165]

The point of departure in his legal thinking is that Islam is the religion of nature (*Al Fitra*) and the religion of the future. The Islam he was talking about was that of the Qur'an, the great Prophet as derived from his life and Tradition, and from the life of his righteous successors and the learned amongst his Companions.[166] He saw modern civilisation to be leading towards Islam. Was this a true conviction on his part or was it a simple rationalisation for his infatuation with Europe and its civilisation? (He often repeated that he visited Europe to regain his spiritual strength.)[167] The obvious contradiction between Islam and modern society sprang, according to him, from the rigidity of the Muslims. This rigidity in the precepts of the Shari'a caused difficulties, which made the people neglect it.

In the days of true Islam the Shari'a was tolerant to the point of encompassing the whole world. Today it is so narrow even for its own people that they are forced to adopt other laws and to seek the protection of their rights outside it. Even the learned and the pious take their disputes to laws other than their own.[168]

The neglect of the Shari'a was further attributed by him to ignorance. He observed that only very few knew anything about it. In consequence it had lost its hold on the mind of the general public because of their inability to apply its precepts to their lives and 'the most important barrier in the way of its application is the inability to understand its laws because of the difficult language used and because of the diversity of opinions.'[169] Unlike many apologists,' Abduh did not think that differences of opinion amongst Muslim jurists were a source of mercy. He conceived Muslim law as one based on the original sources and allowing for no schools. His opinion of the schools and their founders was that they were not binding on any Muslim.

The words of the Imam Mujtahid, that is the founder of a school, should not be elevated to the rank of religion. This is against Islam itself and those who do it commit what Allah warned against. They would have followed in the steps of the people of the Book about whom the Qur'an says, 'They took the learned and the monks to be their Gods in place of God.'[170]

He regarded the Shari'a to consist of two major parts. One part consists of clearly stated laws which every Muslim must know and abide by. These laws are clearly stated in the Holy Book and explained in detail in the Prophetic Tradition, and have been transmitted from one generation of Muslims to another through practice. They are indisputable laws agreed to by everyone (that is supported by *Ijma'*). There is no room, regarding them, for individual independent thought. The second part consists of rules not derived from clear-cut texts nor supported by consensus and, therefore, a subject for independent thought. This type does not concern general rules of rituals or prohibitions, but it touches upon details of these aspects of religion and also upon the relationship between individuals (*mu'amalat*).[171] He advises that Muslims, if learned, should seek the evidence for each ruling, taking guidance only from the works of the early scholars. Their action, however, must accord with their own personal judgement. Laymen should consult with a person whom they can trust in matters of this nature. In this connection, 'Abduh quotes Malik as saying that all rituals must accord with the text without attempt at any interpretation. Mu'amalat, on the other hand, where there is no clear text, should hinge on the interest of the public. According to this position the Muslim jurist is given a greater freedom than the traditionalists accorded him. Consequently Muslim society is accorded the same degree of liberty to develop its own laws in accordance with the principle of utility. In practice, however, 'Abduh never digressed from the beaten track of earlier scholars, and his advice to the authorities regarding the reform of the Shari'a courts was that the judge in these courts should not be tied to one school of thought but should be allowed to use his own opinion in applying the most suitable ruling without restriction to a particular school. He further, in contrast with his contemporaries, clearly states that wholesale prohibitions — common in those days of everything European — are not based on Muslim law. The early scholars such as Shafi'i and Abu Yusuf and the learned among the Companions of the Prophet never adjudged anything to be prohibited unless it was so clearly stated in the Holy Book that it needed no further explanation.[172]

In combating the narrow views of Muslim law, 'Abduh resorted to the old scholars to support his more liberal views. He was able through the device of *Talfiq* on the one hand and the consideration of public interest on the other to justify some of the new institutions which his contemporaries initially ignored. In the economic sphere he legalised shareholdings and the taking of interest on savings in the post office.[173] Among his Muslim contemporaries he was one of the first to recognise the problem of a plural society which was imposed upon the largely 'closed' Muslim society.

Although 'Abduh's political and other quarrels contributed a great deal to linking his name in many Muslim circles with extreme liberalism, the truth of the matter is that 'Abduh was up against a traditional society that derived security and certainty from its long social isolation and its established habits. Once this isolation ended, the habits derived from it became pointless or even harmful. The *Ulema* were not, however, ready to discard them. On the contrary, they declared them inviolate. The Transvaal Fatwa, for instance, resulted from the new situation in which Muslims had to come into contact on a much wider basis than previously with non-Muslims, a situation which had not taken place since the earliest times of Islam. 'Abduh found for the legitimisation of greater intercourse between Muslims and other societies: he was bound to do so not only because it was inevitable, but also because he regarded the interest of Muslims to be precisely in the continuation and growth of contact with others.

'Abduh contributed to the reform of the Shari'a courts. His proposals, particularly those bearing on the administrative side, were urgently needed and adopted. His theoretical position, namely giving equal authority to all schools of law, was much slower in establishing itself. Jurists, however, found themselves, under the pressure of modern society, driven into defending Muslim law by the use of all schools, even the less recognised ones. This device, as shall be pointed out later, became a standard in the literature of Shari'a apologetics.

Naturally 'Abduh wished the maze of Egyptian justice in its numerous law systems and diversities of thought to be absorbed in one system of law, the Shari'a. He was, however, aware that with the power in the hands of a non-Muslim country, Britain, such a hope was well nigh impossible. He therefore secretly struggled (according to him) to protect the Shari'a courts, against what he thought to be Cromer's secret intention to abolish them,[174] through the appointment of two civil judges to the High Shari'a Court. Although he saw clearly the defects of Al Azhar and the shortcomings of the courts of the time, he insisted on the continuation of the link between Al Azhar and these judicial institutions. Only

when he failed in his efforts to reform Al Azhar did he turn
to the idea of establishing an alternative institution. He
would not have the 'School of Law' as a substitute. His
suspicion of the Western-oriented institutions remained
powerful. He put forward a project for the establishment of a
school for Shari'a law (Madrassat Al-Qada' Al Shar'i) insisting
that though it could be linked to Al Azhar as he wished it
must remain under the authority of the Mufti.[175] He died
before the project was to materialise. When it was established
later, the school performed its function for a number of
years, but under the pressure of Al Azhar, whose leadership
later agreed to the introduction of a number of reforms, the
school was abolished in favour of an institute within Al
Azhar.

'Abduh's legal reforms, at least in their practical application, depended on the adoption of his reforms by Al Azhar.
As Al Azhar failed for the reasons mentioned above, his
legal reforms outside the administrative ones materialised
only gradually, largely because of the transformation of
Egyptian society. Undoubtedly 'Abduh paved the way for
the liberal-minded to follow, but one is bound to wonder
whether his methods and his personality did not constitute
a greater obstacle in the way of reform than need be.

Early in his career, 'Abduh viewed the law as reflecting
the mentality of the people, their customs and traditions.
It is natural, therefore, that it should differ from place to
place and from one period of time to another. He was aware
that laws do not change people, but 'only reflect the faculties
which members of the community have acquired through its
common practices and customs'.[176] He makes it clearer by
stating that the laws are not the instrument 'which educate
nations and improve their condition. Laws everywhere in the
world are made only for the abnormal and the mistakes and
faults. The laws which reform the people are those of education based on religion for every nation.'[177] During this period
he was speaking of the law in general terms. It was during his
liberal nationalist phase. He, however, continued to hold
these views and reconciled them with the doctrine of the
finality of the Shari'a. He said 'The Islamic Shari'a is universal and eternal. A corollary of this is that the Shari'a suits

the interests of humanity at every time and in any place whatever the nature of the civilisation. A Shari'a of such a nature, its specific items cannot be limited because it deals with the affairs of the people wherever they are.'[178] He stresses the changing nature of the detailed items of the Shari'a in contrast to the permanent nature of its general principles.

Contrasting his views on the role of customs in relation to the Shari'a with his views on the role of reason in the discovery of ethical principles,[179] one is bound to see a contradiction of a serious nature. In discussing man's ability to discover unaided by revelation the moral law which accords with the nature of the actions, 'Abduh appeared to subscribe to the rationalist ethics of Descartes.[180] Custom and convention are not regarded as reliable sources in the rationalist system. As is known, the Shari'a is not only a legal system but also an ethical one. It appears, therefore, that 'Abduh appeals to reason when discussing the theory of value and to custom and convention when considering the actualities of life. He thus subscribes to absolutism in theory and relativism in practice.

'Abduh's Impact on Egyptian and Muslim Thought

No Egyptian in modern times has been so highly regarded as 'Abduh, both in Egyptian and foreign circles.[181] It is important in assessing his contribution to the development of Egyptian and Muslim thought to see him in proper perspective. He emerged in an Egypt faltering under the impact of European cultural influences. He was fortunate in meeting the indomitable Al-Afghani who introduced him to Western culture and instilled in him ideas of liberty and political reform. Like all major Muslim thinkers, Sufism is the foundation of his ethical life and outlook. The rebellion against the orders and the revulsion of their doctrine, characteristics of modernism in general, was not against Sufism *per se* but against the corruption and decadence of its institutions in the nineteenth century.[182] He always recognised the Sufis as the incomparable teachers of ethic. He considered their decline to be the major cause for the decline of Islam.[183] He blamed the jurists for the plight of Sufism. It was under the jurists' pressure that the Sufis resorted to symbolism which obscured their true principles. This led to the ignorance of the true nature of Sufism and the decline of Islam. The jurists were no substitute for the Sufis. They lacked *Tasawwuf*, 'which is the true religion'. In consequence they were ignorant of the politics and general conditions of their day. For this reason they were unable to implement the rules of the Shari'a.[184] He points out that the jurists, unlike the Sufis, were a tool in the hands of the political arm of the state. As such, they were regarded with contempt by the rulers upon whom they were unable to exert any influence. He suggested as a remedy the abandonment of ideas of the era of decline in favour of the old masters. Again it was the same call: 'Let's go back to true Sufism in the days of its inception.'[185]

The effect of his attitude to the Sufis, however, was more destructive than constructive. The trend towards modernity in Muslim society militates against the Sufi orders, but 'Abduh and the Salafis offered an added and more powerful argument against them, an argument based upon religion. The decline in Sufi prestige and influence had immense consequences for Egypt. As shall be pointed out later, the emergence of religious societies or even political parties was at least in part caused by this decline. The function performed by the Sufi orders both in the social life of the individual and in his emotional and religious activities were left without a substitute. The sense of belonging, the social cohesion, the emotional satisfaction, the depth of religious feelings and experience, and above all the sense of security derived from the concept of an ordered and paternalistic society had its foundation disturbed or even destroyed.

'Abduh's major failure derives from his lack of adequate response from the Muslim community. In his thought he addressed the West more than he did his fellow Muslims. He appeared to many of his contemporaries, and to some of the generation after, more as a follower of Europe than as an exponent of Islam.[186]

If 'Abduh's contribution to the weakening of the Sufi orders[187] can be considered significant, his influence upon legal thinking was limited, for in the first place his sweeping proposals evoked suspicion that his limited and restrained application of them did not mitigate. We have observed earlier that he remained always within the framework of the schools of law. At no time could any competent jurist find fault with his judgements. Perhaps at the practical level he was able to recognise the fact that the stage of development in Muslim society at that time did not warrant the sweeping reforms that he suggested.[188] On the other hand, his failure to put his principles into actual practice may be an indication of his fear of the consequences. He, however, had a forceful ally, namely modernity. And it is not surprising that his supporters were drawn mainly from those exposed to Western culture.

The party of 'Abduh, as Rashid Ridha called them, or the Girondists of Egypt, as Cromer chose to name them, were a group of friends, most of whom were deeply immersed in Western ideas. They gathered around 'Abduh probably because they found with him a satisfaction which the conservatives could not provide and a sense of identity which the Western masters were clearly incapable of giving. This party of 'Abduh was in reality more Western than Muslim. The activities of Lufti Ali-Sayyid, the chief theoretician of the party, and his contributions only go to prove this. The impact of the ideas he advocated on the Egyptian masses was negligible. Lufti Ali-Sayyid, despite the grand title of 'The Teacher of the Generation', was always regarded more as a translator of Aristotle than as a leader of political or social thought.[189]

As a good number of the party of 'Abduh grew into the party of the West a cleavage appeared amongst his alleged disciples. His chief student and disciple Rashid Ridha grew disenchanted with the group that in 1907 he had regarded as the Hope of Egypt.[190] 'Abduh's compromise between modernity and Islam could be seen therefore to have at least in the social sense failed. The Western wing of his supposed friends became more Western, while the Muslim wing became, in a manner of speaking, more Muslim.

The emergence of Sa'd Zaghlul after the First World War was regarded by Rashid Ridha as a victory for 'Abduh, and is so assessed by various other writers.[191] But it is important for us to realise that the militant nationalist in Zaghlul leads back directly to Al-Afghani rather than to 'Abduh.[192] In a sense Zaghlul took the position of Mustafa Kamil, the arch-opponent of 'Abduh, and inherited his tremendous popular support. Like all good ambitious politicians, Zaghlul identi-fied himself with the most popular trend. He was aware, like many nationalists the world over, that oppressive rule was no longer feasible in the colonies and that he could with impu-nity challenge British power. The victory of the Wafd in popular terms and its success in forcing a British retreat can-not possibly be related to the passive and co-operative poli-cies of 'Abduh. On the other hand, the party's secular nationalist programme owes more to the Westernisers than to 'Abduh's strict Muslim principles (in his last phase).

In the educational field 'Abduh's proposals were outdated by the rapid development of Egypt. His failure in Al Azhar created in that institution a hardened reaction against reform. It was not until 1928 that a member of his school was brought into the office of Rector of that institution. His resignation a short time afterwards was the best indication of the strength and depth of the opposition to 'Abduh and his ideas.[193]

The slow development of Al Azhar reflected the actual developments of Muslim society in Egypt. Despite the trap-pings of a Western-style government, the Egyptian village remained under a medieval authoritarian rule. Western-type schools, being always city-centred, left the village almost un-touched. It is a fact that Al Azhar, though situated in the town, drew the bulk of its students and exercised the greatest influence in the rural areas. The transformation of Al Azhar presupposes the transformation of the Egyptian village, a fact that 'Abduh and his students never recognised and in conse-quence their influence was limited.

Probably the most important contribution of 'Abduh was that he offered to some Western-educated a road to Islam which the conservatives were unable to do. In so doing he may have delayed the movement of complete secularisation which was inherent in Westernisation. On the other hand, the immense literature about religion which appeared through his activities enriched Egyptian thought and helped to bring into focus a number of controversial social questions.[194]

The problem of the position of the Muslim woman, her inevitable progress towards emancipation, was given sanction by 'Abduh himself on various occasions.[195] But it was a member of his circle, Qassim Amin, in his famous book *Tahrir al-Mar 'ah (The Emancipation of Women)* who attacked Muslim treatment of women as being in violation of Islam itself. The violent reaction that this book evoked was indicative of the state of society at the time. It was the first specific proposal in a matter of social and legal import that the circle of 'Abduh put forward. Both Rashid Ridha and Lufti Al-Sayyid inform us that 'Abduh witnessed the development of the ideas of the book.[196] The gradual emancipation of the Egyptian woman, however, did not result from the arguments of Qassim Amin. It took place as a consequence of the growth of modern economic and cultural institutions despite the opposition of the main stream of 'Abdists.[197]

Even Qassim Amin himself shows the intensity of the conflict between Islam and Western concepts. His first book sought to prove that the freedom of the woman was the intention of the Shari'a; his second, *Al Mar'ah Al jadidah*, ignored the Shari'a altogether and drew its concepts from the West.[198] The critics of 'Abduh were obviously apprehensive of such a development. They clearly regarded 'Abduh as the Trojan Horse of Westernisation.

Despite the alienation of the two wings of 'Abduh's friends, both sides held him in veneration and reverence; but as events in Egypt moved and the cleavage sharpened, the confusion about the true nature of 'Abduh's thought and ideas became more acute.[199] Rashid Ridha and the Manarists were led into a fundamentalist position so close to the position of Ibn Taimiya that they found common cause with the Wahhabis.[200] It is true that 'Abduh never criticised the Wahhabis except with regard to their excessive enthusiasm in supporting their ideas.[201] Their fanaticism rather than their theological position constituted for 'Abduh their main shortcoming, but the care that 'Abduh had always taken in making his ideas less precise and less committed than might be, together with his mode of life and almost certainly enlightened though unwritten views, contributed to the liberal image that has always been painted of him in Westernised circles.[202]

In the field of literature and the development of the Arabic language, 'Abduh together with the other students of Al-Afghani was responsible for the literary movement that emerged in the closing years of the last century and the early years of this. 'Abduh, following a cue from Al-Afghani and conscious of the importance of the classical age as a source of inspiration and as a guide in the difficult circumstances of the Muslim world, was instrumental in reproducing the old classical words in various fields; but like many other things in the life of 'Abduh, the young plant which he nursed was taken over by the Westernisers and brought up to be a vastly different one from what he intended, if indeed his intentions could be ascertained. The Arabic that in the time of Al-Jabert could not convey the idea of a republic[203] was made by this school and the following generation an adequate vehicle for Western as well as eastern ideas. Thus Arabic, freed from the shackles of medieval formalism and modes of thought, developed into a meaningful activity reflecting and influencing the ideas of the modern Arab and the modern Muslim.

His role in the 'Urabi rebellion is not yet clear. His early equivocation and later enthusiasm did not endear him to either party.[204] His writing about the affair may have been motivated by factors other than the desire to proclaim the truth.[205] One must hesitate in agreeing with Cromer's assessment of him as 'one of the leading spirits of the movement'.[206] The ideas that were influential then and the writers who were prestigious belonged to various sources and schools of thought.[207] His studied reasonableness and his comparative lack of emotion must have deprived his articles of much influence, especially those dealing with political problems. Only where he referred to the Ministry of Education did he show that aggressiveness characteristic of Al-Afghani's style.[208] Doubtless this contributed to the favourable reaction of the administration.

During his work with Al-Afghani he forcefully put their ideas in the periodical *Al 'Urwat*, which to this day remains one of the most influential periodicals in the history of modern Islam.[209] It was his image as the collaborator of Al-Afghani that his apologists resort to when defending his later co-operation with Cromer.[210] The latter period of his life was, however, the period of maturity in thought and greater concentration on academic work. It was also the period during which he aroused the greatest suspicion with regard to his political and religious views. Probably his most famous contribution during the age of maturity was his *Tafsir*, which is characterised by its concern for the practical, social problems and the attempt to arrive at the simplest and most direct meaning of the revelation.[211] Exegesists ever since have found it necessary to relate the Qur'an to the problems of everyday life.

'Abduh attempted to play the role of the political leader without its qualifications and sought to fulfil the function of a religious reformer but without adequate tools. The result was a thought marred by eclectic tendencies and preoccupation with the practical consequences of his ideas.[212] Despite this the name of 'Abduh grew in prestige as time went on. No doubt the reason for this was mainly Rashid Ridha and *Al Manar*.[213] 'Abduh the man may have been noticed by the historians of modern Islam as an important if not great figure, but 'Abduh the myth is a compelling and considerable force. *Al Manar* spread his name throughout the Muslim world and Rashid Ridha as his public relations officer explained away his faults and magnified his virtues. The imitators of *Al Manar* followed it into calling 'Abduh Al Ustaz Al Imam and holding him as an undisputed authority. One must wonder whether the various commemorative functions for 'Abduh would have been held had it not been for the moving spirit of Rashid Ridha. In a society of which 'Abduh himself lamented the incapacity to honour its great men it is surprising that so much honour has been bestowed upon him.

Outside Egypt, in India and Malaysia, Tunisia and Algeria, 'Abduh's name and more so the ideas associated with it exerted great influence on modern developments. The Muhammadiyyah[214] of Indonesia was inspired by his interpretation of Islam.

Muhammad 'Abduh as a Thinker

In his autobiography, 'Abduh states his objective as being two important matters:

> the first is to liberate the minds from the chains of imita-
> tion, to understand religion in accordance with the ways of
> the Salaf before the appearance of disputes, and the return
> to its primary sources to acquire religious knowledge, and
> to consider religion as one of the controls over human
> reason which God has meant for guiding it away from
> error so that the will of Allah in preserving mankind may
> be fulfilled, therefore religion is a friend of science and a
> stimulus towards research into the secrets of the world,
> calling for the respect of the established facts . . . In this
> matter I deviated from the two great groups who consti-
> tute the Umma, the students of religion and the students
> of modern disciplines. The second was the reform of the
> style of the Arabic language . . .[215]

The intellectual task that 'Abduh set for himself is thus specified; to simplify Islam through the return to its early stages and thus allow for a place beside it for science and modern knowledge. The first, namely simplification, is a task that is much more difficult than is at first sight realised. It means more than shedding of ideas and solutions to questions. It meant in reality the rejection of some of the questions themselves.[216] 'Abduh's criteria for a valid question was that it had practical implications and that it was derived directly from the sources and does not emerge from pure speculation. Thus the rationalist was on this score an anti-rationalist. Historically, as we have observed, 'Abduh moved from Sufism through rationalism to the attitude of the Salafia school.

There was no consistent principle underlying his thought. He formed no philosophical system.[217] But his ideas were eclectic in nature with greater inclination if no public objection took place to the views of the Mu'tazilah.[218] He adopted the puritanical and fundamentalistic views of Ibn Taimiya, and also took over the ethical values of Ghazali. Further, he attempted to incorporate and fuse into religious knowledge some aspects of modern science as he was able to understand it.[219] The mixture aroused more suspicion than confidence in 'Abduh's intentions and even his sincerity.[220]

In the assessment of A. Hourani, 'Abduh effected a balance between Islam and modernity.[221] But one wonders whether this balance was not more illusory than real. In 'Abduh's view the conflict between religion and science arose from the rigidity of the religious officials, indeed rigidity which afflicted all spheres of the Muslim community. But he felt that once this rigidity disappears, and it must disappear, then they will find the Qur'an waiting for them, 'preparing the means of salvation and supporting them through it with a holy spirit and taking them into the sources of science'.[222]

Does 'Abduh, therefore, consider religious truth to be also dynamic and unstable as that of science? Hardly: he could scarcely subscribe to such a view and Osman Amin errs in assessing 'Abduh as equating religion with science in this respect.[223] Indeed, at every level religion must assert absolutism, or be relegated to the position of mere speculation. Further, religion, even if it permits the modification of certain inessential aspects by science, cannot possibly allow any tempering with its basic principles. 'Abduh was certainly aware that there are certain irreducible elements in Islam. He, however, appeared to think that they did not contradict science.

The final view of Islam emerging from 'Abduh's thought is imprecise, not so much because 'Abduh abhorred Taqlid as A. Hourani suggests,[224] but more likely because his ideas were more in the nature of a programme of action and were not as easily implemented as he thought.

The tension between modernity and Islam was thus obscured and not resolved. Even during his lifetime members of his circle disputed most violently on matters of social policy.[225] The scientific dynamic attitude was not, through his system, projected on religion. On the contrary, the rigid and final attitude of religion was conferred upon science.[226]

The circle of 'Abduh shared a negative attitude to nineteenth-century Islam and a belief in the permanent truth of their faith and its suitability regardless of time and place to be the basis for human progress and happiness. Beyond this general attitude, they differed widely in hue between the conservative Manfaluti to the progressive and liberal Qassim Amin, between the fundamentalist Rashid Ridha and 'the scientific Tantawi Jawhari'.[227]

Underlying 'Abduh's programme was the elimination of disunity within the *Ummah* and alleviating the spiritual crisis contingent on its failure to apply fully the law of Islam. Modern conditions, having brought about foreign institutions in economic, educational, political and social matters, drew the *Ummah* gradually but irresistibly away from traditional and Shari'a precepts. His proposal for unity was to go back to Islam as it was before the disputes. But neither he nor Al-Afghani succeeded in uniting the *Ummah*. On the contrary, they added to its factions a new one. However, the Salafis helped to allay the anguish of the community with regard to its failure to implement the law of God. The principle of utility in Muslim legislation was given a new force by 'Abduh as he declares. 'If a ruling has become the cause of harm, which it did not cause before, we must change it in accordance with the prevailing conditions.'[228] 'Abduh was not alone in voicing these views. He was even less adventurous than his counterpart in India.[229] But as we have noted earlier, a discrepancy between theory and practice is always present in his system. 'Abduh's achievement therefore consists of a method, albeit imprecise, rather than a complete interpretation of Islam. The ambiguity of his ideas served as a cover against criticism. 'Abduh was after all, as Rashid Ridha aptly suggested, a politician who had strayed into religion.[230]

3 MUHAMMAD RASHID RIDHA

Al-Afghani was the inspirer of the Salafiyyah school. 'Abduh was its brains; but Rashid Ridha was its spokesman.[1] He was born in Syria, educated in the traditional manner of the *ulema*, and was accorded the Certificate of 'Alim in 1897.[2] His teacher was one Shaikh Hussain Al-Jisr, a Syrian theologian of distinction. Though the Shaikh was certainly a traditionalist, his book, *Al Resalat Al Hamidiyyah*, in the defence of Islam indicates a change in the attitude of Muslims towards Western opinion on Islam. It is a mark of his breadth of mind that he discussed Darwinism and suggested that if it proved true it need not contradict the Qur'an.[3] There is no doubt that such a teacher must have prepared the minds of his students to the ideas of the more progressive thinkers, such as Al-Afghani and others.

Rashid Ridha indicates that he fell under the influence of Ghazali through his book *Ihiya 'Ulum Al Din (The revival of the religious sciences)*, which led him into taking up some Sufi practices such as refraining from good food and sleeping on the ground; he even attempted to tolerate dirtiness in body and clothes but was unable to do so.[4] In his short notes about his life intended for publication with his book, *Al-Manar wa Al-Azhar*, he relates the many strange experiences he had.[5] During this period he joined the Naqshahbandi Order.[6]

The second book to influence his life was *Al 'Urwat al Wuthqa*, which changed his outlook completely. Before reading it his concern was with his salvation through the right belief and rituals. If his thoughts had ever gone beyond his personal salvation into the more mundane aspects of social life it was concentrated on local reforms, but when he read *Al 'Urwat al Wuthqa* all this was changed. A universal outlook replaced the parochial and the affairs of Islam in general took the place of individual salvation.[7] One effect of his Sufi phase was that he refrained from learning Turkish and French when he had the opportunity in the national school, because he believed then that 'There is no religious use in their study.'[8]

After reading *Al 'Urwat* he started looking for the writings of Al-Afghani and 'Abduh, and all the writings about them. He also became so much a partisan of the two leaders that no one could attack them in front of him. In 1893 he wrote a letter to Al-Afghani requesting to be accepted as a student. The letter contained such praise of Al-Afghani that he proudly showed it to many of his visitors. Ridha apologised for not joining Al-Afghani immediately because he believed 'Constantinople, large as it is, even the Ottoman kingdom in its width has no place for the Sayyid because oriental kingdoms have become like a sick fool who refused medicine simply because it was medicine.'[9]

His intention of joining Al-Afghani was frustrated by the latter's death in 1897, upon which Ridha decided to join 'Abduh. He met 'Abduh in Tripoli in Syria after the latter's return from Europe, and met him a second time in the same place when 'Abduh came on his summer holiday. On this occasion he stayed with him all the time from early morning to bedtime.[10] He later travelled to Egypt to join him. At their first meeting they spoke about the hope for Islamic reform, the reform of Al Azhar and politics, of which 'Abduh expressed his distaste. They also mentioned certain aspects of saint worship which 'Abduh deplored.

After this, and before the publication of *Al Manar*, Rashid Ridha frequented 'Abduh's house to discuss with him various reform problems, taking care to write down a summary of their discussion. He found that they did not differ, 'Except with regard to a few questions which ended after discussion in agreement, such as the question of "Bab and Baha".'[11]

It is important to realise that Ridha, before his immigration to Egypt, had written a book with the title of *Al Hakmat Al Shar'iyyah*, which seems to have impressed many contemporaries by its style and independence of opinion. Among the questions he discussed in the book were, significantly, the harm of the Mahdist outlook which makes Muslims pin their hopes for reform on an outside force, the threat of foreign domination and the question of dress from the point of view of religion, society, ethics and politics.[12]

There is little doubt that Rashid Ridha, before coming to Egypt, was already an accomplished scholar and that the influence of 'Abduh upon him was more of a confirmation than an initiation.

As Ridha intended from the beginning to publish a paper in Egypt he consulted 'Abduh about it. 'Abduh, after a discussion, agreed to the idea and suggested that the paper should not be partisan nor indulge in arguments with other papers and should be independent of the so-called great personalities. Although 'Abduh agreed with the contents of *Al Manar* when it came into being, he was critical of the bluntness of its arguments, the difficulty of its language which put it beyond the scope of the ordinary reader and its involvement in Ottoman politics. It is a measure of 'Abduh's control over the paper that Rashid Ridha states in the preface to the twelfth volume, 'We sometimes wished to indulge in it [politics] but *Al-Ustaz Al-Imam* used to stop us. We did not get what we wanted until after Allah had called him.'[13]

For four years *Al Manar* struggled with a very small circulation and only in the fifth year did it become widely read.[14] The aim of *Al Manar* was to continue the work of *Al 'Urwat Al Wuthqa* in fields other than the 'Egyptian' political field. It aimed at social, religious, political and economic reforms and to prove that Islam as a religion was not incompatible with contemporary conditions and that the Shari'a was still a practical instrument for modern government. On the negative side, it aimed at purifying Islam from prevailing superstitions and combating fatalism, narrow partisanship as regards the schools of law, saint worship and the harmful innovations of the Sufi orders. It aimed also at advocating tolerance and understanding between the various sects, the promotion of public education, the reform of school books and methods of teaching, the encouragement of science and arts and to stimulate the Muslim nations into competing with other nations in matters essential to their progress.[15]

Al Manar republished a number of articles by Al-Afghani and 'Abduh from *Al 'Urwat* and elsewhere which accorded with its policy. From the third year onwards it started publishing the famous *Tafsir Al-Manar*, the encyclopedic work of reformism. In the same year it also started a section for Fatwas, or legal opinion, to advise its readers on questions of shari'a or doctrines. There is no doubt that this last section was utilised by Ridha to disseminate his ideas of legal reform.[16]

For 37 years *Al Manar* was involved in the affairs of the Muslim world, political, religious and social — so much that it has become a record of the development of Islam in a crucial period of its history.

Many Muslims in areas as distant as Morocco and Indonesia read it regularly and correspond with it. It could not refrain from expressing opinions on problems such as the Tijanis in the Maghreb or the Alawis in Indonesia. Although during the life of 'Abduh it turned after a short period from a diagnosis of Muslim ills to putting suggestions to the authorities to effect reform, it found itself having to remind Muslims that mere suggestion without the active participation of the public was futile. In its discussions, style and subject matter it was a journal for a special section of the Muslim community: those who are learned or greatly interested in religious questions.

Most of Ridha's works were serialised in *Al Manar*. The bulk of the contributions in the magazine were the product of his own pen. His relationship with 'Abduh brought him benefits as well as powerful enemies. Among those enemies was Abbas II, whose pathetic efforts to silence him culminated in an address to the Al Azhar *ulema*, in which he suggested that Ridha might just go home.[17] He also earned the undying hatred of the conservative Azharites, and lacking that Western veneer which made 'Abduh so attractive to many Western-educated he was unable to communicate adequately with them. His isolation, which grew more and more acute, was due to these intellectual differences. He belonged neither to Al Azhar's circles nor to their opponents, the Westernisers.

A further reason for his isolation must be found in the fact that, unlike 'Abduh, who was content to leave vague principles alone and to accept what sometimes were contradictory positions, Ridha's personality, his training and strict adherence to the school of Ibn Taimiya drove him into attempting to give precise and definite statements of his position. In matters of religion, nothing calls for enmities more than the attempt to give unequivocal pronouncements on questions that by their very nature must be allowed to remain ambiguous.

At no time did Ridha think or suspect that he was deviating from 'Abduh. He was simply expounding and explaining the views of the master, or so he thought.[18] Still a further cause for his isolation stems from the general development of Egyptian and Muslim society. In the decades following 'Abduh's death the flood gates of Western ideas were opened wide — the upheavals of economic crisis, the Great War and the suddenly discovered ideals of the West as expressed in the Wilsonian principles. The establishment in Egypt in 1908 of a university on Western lines to become intentionally or otherwise a centre for European ideas made education at the higher level no longer (if indeed it had ever been since Muhammad Ali) the monopoly of Al-Azhar. The new university did not only reject the basic assumptions of Al-Azhar, but it challenged the very right of its existence. Rashid Ridha regarded it as the hotbed of heresies.[19]

At the social and political level Ridha acted as a foreigner. He attacked the Ottoman Empire and France when the nationalists pinned their hopes on them to dislodge the British out of Egypt. Belonging as he did to the group that befriended Cromer, he was lumped together by the nationalists with the Syrian Christian journalists of Al Muqatam as 'intruders' (Dukhala'). Ridha resented this very greatly and lamented the sort of nationalism which equates an 'Arab and a descendant of the Prophet with a heathen Mongolian or Chinese'.[20] He decried the nationalism of the nationalist party, declaring it against Islam.[21]

A still further, though perhaps less obvious cause for Ridha's isolation was the fact of being a Sayyid. Despite Ridha's objection to the Alawiyyah claim to the supremacy of the descendants of the Prophet, he retained, as shall be pointed out, their basic attitude and envisaged a privileged position for them within the framework of the democratic principles which are 'prevalent nowadays'.[22]

Despite his stay in Egypt for nearly forty years, Rashid Ridha never managed to work his way into the ranks of

Egyptian society. Unlike the Tunisian Shaikh Muhammad Al-Khadr Hussain, who was able to obtain the post as the first editor of the official Al Azhar magazine and some thirty years later to be appointed the Rector of Al Azhar, Ridha maintained a contemptuous attitude towards the whole institution and its products. It seems as if 'Abduh's retreat from Al Azhar was taken by Ridha as a permanent declaration of war. There is no better evidence for his failure to be absorbed within Egyptian institutions than that his friend and fellow disciple of 'Abduh, Mustafa Al-Maraghi, thought it prudent when he became Rector of Al Azhar in 1928, only to consult with Ridha about the reforms in that institution without offering him any post in it.[23] Near the close of his life Ridha became involved in a dispute with one of the traditional *ulema* and took the chance to heap contempt on the entire institution exempting only the few who like him were imbued with Salafi tradition.[24]

Rashid Ridha's Legal Reform

The school of Al-Afghani and 'Abduh was concerned at the disparity between Muslim ideal and Muslim reality. At the centre of its aims is the bridging of the gap between the two. In no area of Muslim life was this disparity more manifest than in the field of law. As European influence, cultural and otherwise, grew in strength, European laws were adopted by Muslims, either under the pressure of the Western powers or through the voluntary imposition of the Westernising rulers. In Egypt, Isma'il used the pretext of non-co-operation on the part of the *ulema* in codifying Muslim law to borrow French codes wholesale.[25]

Of course there were areas of the legal system which were borrowed directly from European laws. These areas bore directly on the commercial and certain aspects of international law.[26] No doubt this encourages Muslim rulers to borrow further from the same sources and in certain ways may have softened the resistance to such a procedure.

The purpose and ambition of Al-Afghani and his disciples was to re-establish the Shari'a as the exclusive source of law in Muslim countries. Al-Afghani could simply voice such an opinion in general terms while 'Abduh may be drawn into giving more details of such proposals; but it was left to Rashid Ridha to argue the case.

Ridha starts from the doctrine that

> There is nothing in our religion which is incompatible with the current civilisation, especially those aspects regarded as useful by all civilised nations, except with regard to a few questions of usury [Riba] and I am ready to sanction [from the point of view of the Shari'a] every-thing that the experience of the Europeans before us shows to be needed for the progress of the state in terms of the true Islam. But I must not confine myself to a school of law, only the Qur'an and the authentic Tradition.[27]

This statement formulates the problem, though it was meant to describe the solution. What is the criterion upon which a practice is judged essential to progress? This is left unsaid.

But the statement gives reassurance to the ruling classes, the educated section of the community and to those who wish Muslims to partake in the modern progress that Islam as Ridha perceives it need not be antagonistic to their cherished aim. The task which Ridha set for himself proved difficult and as those who followed him came to realise, much more revolutionary than he thought.

Ridha, like 'Abduh and Al-Afghani, emphasised the need for a continuous Ijtihad, but unlike them he was less tolerant of differences. With his extensive knowledge of the Tradition he was able to discount as untrue the famous Hadith 'Dif-ferences amongst my umma is a source of mercy.'[28] His overriding concern was to show that Islam, the religion of unity, could not possibly commend differences, especially the type of differences which causes antagonism.[29]

He was aware, however, that differences of opinion were natural and must be permitted. The differences in legal matters to which he objected were those which raised the status of the Madzhab to that of religion itself.

> The fanatic partisans of the Madzhabs [schools of law] refuse to make differences of opinion a source of mercy.

Each one of them insists on the necessity of imitating his
own Madzhab without a licence for its followers to imitate
any other, even when it is needed or necessary.[30]

Ridha contrasts this type of partisanship which divided
Muslims over human opinions with the attitude of the
pious forefathers (Salaf Saleh) who tolerated no disunity
amongst Muslims on the strength of individual views.[31] He
further points out that as regards the schools of law, their
founders never claimed such authority for their independent
opinions. The degeneration of the Muslims in the following generations, thinks Ridha, was shown most markedly in
the blind imitation that led them into a position of near
Kufre (unbelief).[32]

Rashid Ridha differentiates between three categories:
doctrines, rituals and rules governing human relationships
(mu'amalat). It is only this third category which permits
of human effort. 'Doctrines and rituals have been perfected
in detail. They are not subject to addition or reduction.
Whoever adds or reduces them is changing Islam and bringing forth a new religion.'[33] Thus Rashid Ridha specifies the
law proper as the subject of any possible reform or change.
The basis of this reform is the interest of the *Umma* in
accordance with the age. This, however, is not to give the
Ummah a free rein, for Islam has determined the principles
of the obligation of virtue such as justice, equality and the
prohibition of aggression, deceit and treachery and specified
certain punishments for certain crimes and instituted the
principle of consultation.' The *Ummah*, through the 'Ulu Al
'Amr from amongst the *ulema* and rulers who must be people
of knowledge and social dignity ['Adalah]' is empowered to
make decisions on matters of detail. They must decide
through consultation 'what is the best for the Umma in
accordance with the times'.[34] He repeats the same idea in
his introduction to Al-Tawfi's treatise on 'Maslaha' (public
interest) to which he gives precedence over the text.[35]

Ridha's statement on this occasion appears more liberal
than any made by him on any other. There, he suggests that
'Mu'amalat [social interaction] revolve in the view of the
Shari'a on the principle of preventing harm and protecting

or effecting what is useful'.[36] He appears to place the principle of utility high above all other principles of jurisprudence. This may have happened under the influence of Al Tawfi. On other occasions Ridha branded as Kafirs Muslims who attempted to implement precisely this idea.[37]It is not surprising, therefore, to find that Rashid Ridha never allowed himself to go that far when it came to specific application.

He describes his position as falling in between two groups, the conservative *ulema* who follow blindly the works of medieval jurists. The other group are those who advise the abandonment of the Shari'a in favour of Western laws.

His group is composed of the moderates who hold that it is possible to revive Islam and to renew its true guidance through following the Qur'an, the authentic Tradition and the guidance of the Al Salaf Al saleh (the pious forefathers). The works of the leaders of the various schools of law are to be taken not as binding but simply as helpful in formulating our own opinions. They also believe that it was possible to reach a compromise between Islam and the best in modern civilisation as the second group wishes. They even believe that religion and civilisation are 'two friends who always agree and never differ'.[38]

Rashid Ridha was aware of the inherent danger in the twin call of his party to a new Ijtihad and strict adherence to the Salaf Saleh. He noted that some people have bestowed upon themselves the dignity of Mujtahids and interpreted the Qur'an without due consideration to its language or to the context. Since they were motivated by the desire to show identity between Islam and modern civilisation, they found it convenient to dismiss the Tradition altogether so as not to be encumbered by it. On the other side of the fence there were those who called themselves Traditionalists and adhered to the apparent meaning of every word reputed to have come from the Prophet. Being ignorant of the nature and the sciences of the Tradition they made no distinction between the categories of Sanads (chain of narrators) nor did they know the differences between what is authentic and what is false. Nevertheless, they branded any doubter of their position as Kafir (unbeliever) or a Fasiq (heretic).[39]

Rashid Ridha thus felt it essential to specify his programme and the principles upon which it is based. He declares that his moderate reformist party regards the Qur'an to be the word of Allah and to be binding on every Muslim and that every expression which bears only one meaning must be so accepted and complied with. On the other hand, if it is capable of different interpretations then it is subject to the efforts of interpretations by qualified people.[40] This is the first principle. We must note here that by insisting that: (a) the clear and unambiguous verses must not be tampered with; and (b) that ambiguous verses must be left to the trained people to interpret and explain. Ridha was pointing out the objections, or some of them, to the ultra modernists who without any training twisted the meaning even of the unambiguous texts.

The second principle is the acceptance of the Tradition of the Prophet in general terms for its rejection would entail with it the very rejection of the Qur'an itself and of Islam.[41] This, however, does not mean that every single Tradition must be accepted. A Tradition related by a single chain (Hadith Ahad), for instance, is only binding on the person who accepts it as authentic, but it need not be made a general rule to which the *Ummah* must adhere.[42]

The third principle is that of the Ijma' (consensus of opinion). In the view of Rashid Ridha only the Ijma' of the first epoch, providing its subject was unquestionably known to the Companions of the Prophet (Ma'lum bi al Dharurah), is binding on everyone. It was through such an Ijma' that the details of Muslim rituals and many aspects of the Shari'a reached us. Hence it would be tantamount to rejecting most aspects of Islam not to rely on their Ijma'. The individual Ijtihad of the Guided Caliphs, their judgements and political decisions are not to be regarded as part of the religion but simply as a pointer to what a Muslim government should do.[43]

Rashid Ridha, it must be noted, wishes to minimise the requirement for a Muslim so as to allow greater freedom for reform on the one hand, and on the other to keep an open mind with regard to questions of differences between Muslims. He used to say that 'We should support each other in what we agree upon and tolerate each other on what we differ.'[44]

Theoretically, Rashid Ridha frees himself greatly of Fiqh and of Tradition since he rejects the authority of the former altogether and suggests regarding the latter as binding in only a limited sphere. In practice, however, Ridha's programme demands a greater research in and reliance on Tradition and also a re-evaluation of the works of earlier scholars, for though they are not regarded as authorities, they are still regarded as guides. The new Ijtihad of Ridha's was thus tantamount to a revival of the Traditional school of law with a few trimmings to fit modern conditions.[45]

While reiterating the principle that Islam is the most complete system under which man's perfection in faith and life can be realised, Rashid Ridha emphasises that matters outside the strict religious sphere are left entirely to the efforts of man. He draws a distinction between Muhammad the Prophet and Muhammad in his wordly functions. In what Muhammad communicates as revelation his authority is absolute; on the other hand his political, military or worldly decisions not based on revelation are the product of human judgement and are, therefore, subject to error.[46]

Although Ridha took the sphere of doctrine and rituals outside the human endeavour, he was well aware that numerous modifications and innovations in the field of worship and a great deal of complexity and sophistication in the basic beliefs of Islam took place. Ridha, following 'Abduh, considered these aspects to be a source of disunity and a serious deviation from Islam itself. It is not, contends Ridha, for Muslims to use their own opinion to decide for the community what is religiously prohibited and what is permitted. Obedience to the people in authority is confined to worldly not religious matters.[47] Innovation in the affairs of man so long as they do not violate any of the basic aims of the Shari'a are not subject to any prohibition, indeed they may be regarded as obligatory.[48]

Regarding *mu'amalat* (social interaction), Rashid Ridha recognises that from the point of view of the evidence purported to bear on them, they are classified into five categories. The first comprises those aspects with specific texts which cannot be doubted either as to their applicability or authenticity. The second refers to those aspects coming under a general rule either directly or by implication and were considered so by the First Generation. These two categories are outside the sphere of Ijtihad.

The third category is that with uncertain evidence such as a Hadith, which was the subject of dispute between the Companions and the learned; this is the field of human effort and it is naturally a subject of dispute amongst the learned in all ages. Under this category come the rulings on certain aspects of cleanliness (Tahara) which were subjects of differences amongst the Salaf. Similarly the rules arrived at by some of the learned through the use of their own deductive methods from the texts of the Qur'an and the Sunna. These rules should not be regarded as general and no one should be obliged to follow them blindly. Questions relevant to public affairs, such as the rulings of judicial or political nature should be examined by the people of authority (Ulu Al Amr) whose opinion becomes binding.

The fourth category deals with questions of customs or public behaviour, such as the manner of eating, drinking, etc. The Hadiths bearing on them are not regarded as enjoining the Muslims to follow a specific behaviour. It is, however, better, Rashid Ridha suggests, that Muslims should follow their rulings in the interest of unity, providing this does no violence to public or private interest.

The fifth category refers to matters not dealt with by the Prophet (Shari'). No one has the authority to oblige or prohibit on religious grounds a Muslim from doing anything under this category.[49]

As Ridha supports the reliance on both the texts and the human evaluation in accordance with the principle of utility, he subscribed to the middle position with regard to the use of Qias. He rejects the view of Ahl Al-Ra'y, who use it excessively, and the Ahl Al-Zahir who oppose it totally.[50]

Ijma' is also examined by him. He observes that it has often been used by the opponents of reformism to discredit its proponents and to depict them as enemies of the *Ummah* and of the faith. It was therefore natural that the concept should be examined by every reformer.

As a great many practices, religious, social and economic

are venerated in Muslim society on the strength of Ijma', the
reformed who seeks to change them must look into their
basis. Ridha, following early Hanbalis, points out that there
are two types of Ijma': one which is manifested by positive
agreement amongst those concerned; the other is what is
called tacit agreement, where those concerned were not
reported to have objected to a particular practice or ruling
that took place in their day. Ridha rejects the second category as an invalid instrument. He suggests that the absence
of objection is difficult to prove since the absence of a
report of opposition does not necessarily preclude it having
happened. What remains, therefore, is the first category,
and even this is subject to certain reservations. In the first
place it must not violate a religious text such as the Qur'an
or an authentic Tradition and in the second, it must include
all those who should express an opinion on the matter. He
notes that with the exception of the period of the Companions it is impossible to effect any such consensus. Even if
it occurred in another generation, it would have the authority
of a revelation only in relation to that generation. In other
words, the consensus of others stands only for as long as no
other consensus cancels it.

Ridha thus throws very strong doubt on the very existence
of Ijma' in a historical and viable sense except in a few cases
where it acts as supplementary evidence to the Qur'an and/or
the Tradition. The Ijma' of later generations, if it could ever
be proved to have taken place, is not binding on the generations after them.[51]

By looking afresh at the aspects of Muslim law with the
aim of formulating a law more in line with the modern age,
Ridha was able to modify a number of important questions
such as the freedom of belief, the question of interest and
insurance in the Muslim state. It is significant, however, that
he employed not the dynamic principle of utility but the
traditional concept of discovering the intention of the
Shari'a.

In the era of liberty and freedom of thought epitomised
in the eyes of many educated Muslims by Western liberalism,
the question of apostasy in Islam looked very much like a
blot on a faith whose apologists portray it as the religion of

freedom. Jurists are unanimous that a Muslim renouncing Islam is punished by death. The practices of early Muslims in fighting the apostates and the Traditions specifying death for those changing their religion are cited as evidence for this rule. Ridha, however, saw this as an unfounded Ijma'. He rejected the Tradition outright as contradicting a general principle in the Qur'an, namely the Verse 256 Sura 2 which states 'No compulsion in religion'. Rashid Ridha also cites Tradition, reporting the Prophet in other cases as having opposed compelling some Arabs who chose Judaism to become Muslims. He explains that the Wars of Apostasy (Hurub Al-Riddah) which were waged by the Companions as being political in nature, caused not by the simple act of renouncing Islam but by becoming a military and social threat to the community.[52]

On the questions of interest and insurance policies, Ridha decries those jurists who are quick to restrict the financial activities of Muslims, thus leaving these affairs in the hands of non-Muslims and threatening the economic interests of the community. He sees nothing wrong with taking up a life insurance policy.[53] He also decries the jurists' misuse of Qias to extend the area of prohibition on taking interest on capital and suggests that the taking of interest on monies left in the bank or post office does not come under the prohibited Riba.[54]

Although Ridha cites with evident support the views of Al-Tawfi and Al-Shatibi on the use of public interest as a basis for legislation preceding in importance every other basis including the Qur'an,[55] he in practice does not go beyond the texts. This is more evident with questions of social structure, such as the position of the woman in society, the structure of the family and such questions as co-education. Regarding the position of the woman in society, Ridha published a book called *Nida' Illa Al Jins Al Latif (A Call to the Fair Sex)*. His intention in this book was to clarify the position of the Muslim woman from the point of view of the Shari'a. He was anxious to show that the Muslim woman is given more rights and privileges than the woman of civilised societies. In his opinion this is not contradicted by the fact that in Islam a woman must always have a legal guardian 'to give her all she needs to be an honoured virgin, a virtuous wife, a careful mother and a respected grandmother'.[56] In a public discussion with a university female student, Rashid Ridha strongly supported the usual social restrictions on the Muslim woman and later branded the girl who wished for greater freedom to mix with the opposite sex as an apostate.[57] On this issue, Ridha retained and glorified the conservative position throughout his life, with the one exception that he thought women were eligible to political rights, just as men. He does not, however, explain fully his statement on the subject.[58]

He also vehemently rejected any modification of the Shari'a penal law. The thief, he maintained, must be punished in accordance with divine law. No doubt Ridha, despite his liberalism or even radicalism in principles, could not bring himself to violate the basic texts of the Qur'an.[59]

The failure of Ridha to carry out his programme of reform has been attributed by M. Kerr[60] to two reasons. The first concerns the moral prestige of the Shari'a in the traditional society where its modification would come up against social convictions. The second is derived from a conflict in Ridha's own attitudes as both a reformer seeking change and an apologist seeking to prove the Shari'a to be self-sufficient. There might still be another reason, namely the absence of a model upon which to fashion a programme of reform. Early in his career the West, some of whose policies he was ready to accept, was his model. Only certain minor questions such as Riba were, according to him, all that separated the law of Islam from the civilisation of the West. As Europe's prestige declined especially after the First World War, confusion set in. The reformists were thrown back into the certainty of the established system in preference to stepping into unchartered land.

Ijtihad in the Shari'a, Ridha declares, is the only foundation for a Muslim renaissance.[61] His effort in this respect may be regarded as falling short of setting Islam on the way to progress.

Rashid Ridha's Theology

Like 'Abduh, Ridha was essentially a jurist and like him he

was adverse to theological discussions of the type that caused disunity in the *Ummah,* solved no problem, bore no relation to practical life and complicated the simple faith of Islam. The question that attracted him most urgently was the prevailing practices concerning saints (Awliya). He echoed the Wahhabis in their attacks on saint worship. His attacks brought a great deal of opposition from the conservative writers who accused Rashid Ridha of over-zealousness and disrupting the unity of the *Ummah.* It was this question among others that divided him from the conservative wing of the Al Azhar *ulema* and it was his partiality to the Wahhabis which brought about his famous dispute with the Al Azhar magazine (*Nur Al Islam*).[62]

For centuries the preoccupation of Muslim theologians, like Muslim jurists, had been the assurance of Muslim conscience that life as it is lived by Muslims was both legitimate in the eyes of the Shari'a and correct from the point of view of doctrine. They sought to reduce the tension inherent in the disparity between the actual and the ideal, as well as the social conflict arising from the existence of powerful factions by narrowing the gap between opposed poles.[63] Ridha contended that saint reverence to the extent of performing certain rituals regarded as legitimate and calling upon them as mediators between man and God puts the Muslims on a par with the *jahilis.* The power of his argument was not missed by the *ulema;* but whereas his concern was with the purification of Islam, theirs was with the pacification of the minds and hearts of Muslims. It was better in the view of the *ulema* to show a general practice as consistent with Islam than to alienate the whole *Ummah* by condemnation.

Ridha regarded the efforts of early theologians which were still studied in Muslim institutions as irrelevant both to the problems of the time and to strengthening the conviction in Muslim hearts. These works were written for apologetic purposes, not for expounding the doctrines. Further, their arguments were directed at opinions prevailing in their day and age. The modern age is no longer concerned with these opinions and indeed new ideas which need to be dealt with have emerged. There is, therefore, a strong need for a purified Kalam (theology), a Kalam which is divested of irrelevancies, simplified and directed at current problems.[64]

Apart from his numerous articles on questions of doctrine, he published his book *Al Wahy Al Muhamadi* in the defence of Islam. This book he regarded as an improvement on 'Abduh's *Resalat Al Tawhid*.[65] His aim in writing it was to call upon the non-Muslim world to accept Islam. He is convinced that modern civilisation with its hypocrisy and misery and disputations leads nowhere, and that in the end there is no remedy to this situation except in the guidance of Islam, the religion of brotherhood, justice, mercy and peace.[66] He cites 'Abduh as saying,

> The civilised nations of the West will suffer from the troubles of their civilisation and its political decadence to such an extent that they will be forced to seek an outlet; that outlet will be found only in Islam. The Islam of the Qur'an and the Sunna and not that of the theologians and the jurists.[67]

The book involves discussions of questions such as the need for religion which Ridha, following Al-Afghani, considers fundamental.[68] To Rashid Ridha, Islam is the only religion that could possibly be accepted by the civilised West. What bars Europe from adopting Islam, in his view, are the Churches and their propaganda against Islam, the European politicans who have inherited from the Church the same antipathy, and thirdly the Muslims themselves. Their pitiful condition, the decadence of their governments and nations, their utter ignorance of their religion and their worldly interests deter others from sharing with such backward people a belief which is held responsible for their ills. He agrees with Al-Afghani that this was the greatest obstacle between Europe and Islam.[69]

The book also deals with the problem of revelation (Wahy), prophecy and the need for it side by side with reason and acquired knowledge. The chapter dealing with these problems was added only with the second edition, perhaps because it was necessary as an introduction to the major issue of proving the prophethood of Muhammad. His method of supporting the prophecy of Muhammad is not the traditional one of enumerating real or imagined miracles but, according to his views, the scientific and logical procedure. He considers miracles and other types of extraordinary happenings as more likely to deter people from accepting Islam.[70]

The second major problem with which the book deals is the Qur'an itself. He deals with it as a miracle and as a factor in the social and religious transformation of Muslims. He suggests that the aims of the Qur'an in social and political reform are achieved by the unity of mankind in the religion of the Shari'a, the religious brotherhood, nationality, language and judicial law.[71]

Although the book is apologetic in nature, it does not follow the usual trend of complete falsification of history. He strongly disapproves of those who seek to attribute to Islam aspects of modern civilisation in the face of historical evidence. He thus points out that slavery was legalised in Islam, but freeing the slaves was the final goal of the faith.[72] His views on war are that Islam is basically peaceful, unless attacked or the efforts of its missionaries are obstructed. Although legitimising war, Islam greatly humanised it both in its application and its aim. The idea of Jihad therefore is modified into a simple method of defence, for even in victory the Muslims, according to Ridha, are not permitted to compel the people of the Book to adopt Islam.[73]

Rashid Ridha's concept of causality deviates, or so he believes, from the general trend in the Ash'ari school. Like Al-Afghani and 'Abduh, he accepts without question that such a relationship exists and he rejects the traditional view that denies it.[74] In his opinion, Al-Ghazali also subscribed to the same views. He recalls his emancipation from the Ash'ari outlook before adopting the position of the Hanbalis. He says,

At the beginning of our study of Kalam we used to see in the [Ash'ari] books the views of the Hanbalis reported, and from this we used to think that they were fundamentalists taken up by the letter of the Revelation without truly understanding it. They did not appear to have known the facts of science or to have related them to the religious texts. In our view the Ash'ari books alone were the source of religion and the path to certainty. Then we had a look at the books of the Hanbalis, and to our surprise we found them the true guide to the ideal path of the Salaf.

He continues in this vein to describe the difference between the Hanbalis and the Ash'arites as that between 'He who walks the straight path and he who swims into a stormy sea buffeted by the waves of philosophical doubt.'[75]

The use of science and logic in place of miracles in religious arguments, the acceptance of the law of causality and the opposition to the practices connected with saints drove Ridha logically into denying the possibility of miracles after the Prophet. He might also have been prompted by the desire to nullify the claims to sainthood; the basis of which among the common people is the Karamats performed by the saints.

He derived this from 'Abduh's own concept of the evolution of man and religion. In 'Abduh's view Islam, unlike Judaism and Christianity, addressed human minds without attempting to overwhelm them emotionally through miracles. Although 'Abduh never goes so far with his conclusions, it is a logical step. His position can lead to the view that the age of miracles has ended as man has matured and the Prophets have been sent. 'Abduh, while accepting the possibility of Karamats, saw no reason for a Muslim to accept every or any particular claim. Rashid Ridha went further to claim that Muhammad ended the age of miracles (Karamats) as well as prophethood.[76]

It was his conviction that in the age of science the less miraculous is the more acceptable, and he thought that had the Qur'an not contained reports of miracles it would have found ready acceptance from many 'open minded Europeans'.[77] It must not be concluded, however, from this position that Rashid Ridha subscribed to a rationalist interpretation of Islam within the limits of the texts. His denial of Karamats, apart from its importance in his argument against saint practices, was essentially apologetic, the main purpose of which was to show the 'scientific' nature of Islam. It did not bar him from accepting such beliefs as the evil eye, for instance.[78] As there were traditions supporting this belief and as it did not appear to Ridha to contradict any of his main principles and more importantly as it was part and parcel of his cultural background, he accepted it without a discussion. The rationalism of Rashid Ridha is therefore a rationalism limited by a specific aim to a specific sphere.

Rashid Ridha's Views on Education

The Salafi school, especially 'Abduh and Ridha, regarded education as the main instrument of social change. Rashid Ridha subscribed to the views of Al-Afghani and 'Abduh regarding the adoption of science and technology and, like them, he stressed the importance of religion in the educational system. He was critical of the Egyptian educational system which aimed at 'preparing youth for the services of the government instead of aiming at training in itself'. He was also critical of the school curricula for its lack of proper care with regard to religious education.[79]

Rashid Ridha, like 'Abduh, concerned himself less with education in general and more with religious education. Although Al-Manar had from its early days a special section for education and carried the translation of Jean-Jacques Rousseau's *Emile*, Ridha's positive contribution to educational thought is best represented by the syllabus he designed for his school, the school for 'propogation and guidance' (Madrassat Al Da'wah Wa Al Irshad).

The idea for this school may have been inspired by 'Abduh, who claimed to have suggested something on this line to Al-Afghani when they were in Paris. The school was aimed at training two classes of people: the *murshids* (guides) who would work within the Muslim community to guide it into the right path and to combat religious deviation,[80] and the *du'ah* (the propagators) who would carry the mission to the non-Muslims.[81]

Although the two types go over basically the same courses, the emphasis differs in accordance with the functions of each. The murshids were to be more concerned about guiding the already convinced to the proper religious behaviour and conviction, whereas the *du'ah* were to be concerned with the defence of Islam against non-Muslims and against the heterodox factions. It is important to note that Rashid Ridha felt it essential that his students should study the actual situation of Muslims and not simply the ideal in the Muslim texts. He, for instance, feels that the study of Tasawwuf should include a social study of the Tariqas, their differences, influence and the factors assisting or hindering their spread. This study, he suggested, should be done side by side with comparison between the ideology of the Tariqas and the teachings of the Prophet.[82]

He includes in his programme international law and the laws governing companies, trade unions and similar organisations, and was not averse to using European authors.[83] Beside the religious subjects, he introduced psychology, sociology, biology, introductory mathematics, hygiene, geography and economics.[84] He also suggested perhaps for the first time in Egypt a proper study of the Bible and the history of the Church.[85]

The school was rightly described as 'a college in which all the disciplines normally taught in colleges are catered for, in addition to religious education and more attention to the Islamic sciences'.[86]

The student body consisted of young men (aged between twenty and twenty-five) belonging to various Muslim nations. Although the school had to close down at the beginning of the First World War, it could count amongst its graduates such luminaries as Sayyid Amin Al Husaini, the Grand Mufti of Jerusalem, Shaikh Yusuf Yassin, the prominent Saudi official, in addition to other leaders of thought in India, Malaysia and even Egypt.[87]

The education of women in the opinion of Rashid Ridha is essential. He, however, considers that the function of the woman in society is different from that of the man and therefore her education must also be different. He subscribes, as has been noted earlier, to the segregation of the sexes and objects most strongly to the movement for co-education in Egypt.[88]

Rashid Ridha's Political Thought

The West provided twin challenges to Egyptian society.

On the one hand, it shook the foundations of its stability and forced it into a re-examination of its basic assumptions. On the other it compelled it to adopt many institutions which did not grow within its own environment.

The Al-Afghani-'Abduh school was brought into existence in answer to this challenge. Believing as they did that Western progress and might sprang from its political and social organisation, they sought to reconstruct Muslim ideals in a way to permit the internalisation of Western forms. What they specifically aimed at was a Muslim society which enjoyed all the advantages of the West. 'Abduh and Al-Afghani advanced as a central principle that Islam and modernity can both form the necessary synthesis for the dynamic and strong Muslim society which they hoped to construct. In Islam that society would find its identity, the cement to its unity and the motive force for its achievement, whereas modernity would provide the instruments of power. Both 'Abduh and Al-Afghani rejected any suggestion of contradiction between the two elements, Islam and modernity. The history of antipathy between religion and science in the European environment was regarded by both as provincial in nature. Islam, they both contended, was different from Christianity in precisely those points where it clashes with modernity. Since modernity was presumed to have its basis in reason it was the preoccupation of the school to prove the rationalism of Islam.

The political liberalism of the West, and particularly French constitutionalism,[89] exercised a great deal of attraction to Muslims in the nineteenth century. Both 'Abduh and Al-Afghani were at some stage advocates of some sort of republican régime. Neither, however, put forward precise formulations. Both men simply appealed to the past, claiming not only its perfection but also its identity with the reforms they now propose. They died before the disappearance of the Ottoman Caliphate. The practical considerations of its existence on the one hand and the external threat to the *Ummah* on the other forced Al-Afghani to take the Sultan Abdul Hamid II as his ally. As for 'Abduh, after 1889 his pen, if not his tongue, kept largely silent on the matter.[90]

Rashid Ridha, however, died much later (1935) than his two intellectual forerunners. He thus witnessed the upheavals leading to, and consequent on, the First World War. Being a Syrian with direct experience of Turkish tyranny and probably less emotional involvement in the Egyptian dilemma than a native Egyptian, he was able to chart a course for himself unhampered by strict loyalty to the Sultan or fanatical concern with British occupation of Egypt. He was consequently accused whether justly or otherwise of being a party to many conspiracies against the Sultan and of cooperation with the British enemies.[91]

In Egypt under the British, Turkey and the Caliph were regarded together with France as the counterpoise for Britain. The Nationalist Party of Mustafa Kamil sought all along to exploit the ambiguous position of British power in Egypt and the unreal suzerainty of the Sultan of Turkey over Egypt to weaken British influence in the country. An attack on the Caliph therefore was seen in nationalist circles as a betrayal of the national cause. Both 'Abduh and Rashid Ridha suffered under the suspicion of disloyalty to the supreme head and most projects they sponsored were met with strong resistance since they were seen as the instruments of British machinations.[92]

The upheavals consequent upon the defeat of Turkey in the First World War and the imminent end of the Ottoman Caliphate brought the whole questions of the Imamate into focus.

In India, the Muslim leader Abou Al-Kalam Azad published a series of articles on the Caliphate from the point of view of Islam in his magazine *Al-Hilal,* which was translated and published in *Al-Manar,* Volumes XXII and XXIII. Among other things, Abou Al-Kalam was calling all Muslims to support the Istanbul Caliph. Azad defended the legitimacy of the Ottoman Caliphate declaring that, though the Sultan was not of Quraish, he was the legitimate Caliph because the Quraishi condition was a violation of the egalitarianism of the Qur'an. Rashid Ridha, who annotated the articles, strongly opposed this view. To him the legitimate Caliph must be a Quraishi one, which in effect meant a Sayyid.[93] His pride as a Sayyid and his belief in the role that the

Sayyids could play in leading Muslim society made him put various suggestions at various times to various authorities or persons to have a Sayyids' university so that the Muslim world might have an educated élite as its leaders.

Rashid Ridha found adequate evidence from the authentic Tradition for this particular attitude, but living as he was in Egypt in the midst of a social and political transformation he was aware that claims based primarily on descent were no longer feasible in the 'democratic age'.[94]

Leaving aside his various activities in the political field both in Egypt, Syria and the Ottoman Empire,[95] his most important political contribution to political thought was contained in his book *Al Khilafa Wal Imama Al Uzma (The Caliphate and the Great Imamate)*.[96] Before its publication in book form it was serialised in *Al Manar,* Volumes XXIII and XXIV (1922-3). He wrote:

> The question of Caliphate and the Sultanate is a source of trouble in Muslim society just as monarchy is a subject of trouble to all other nations. This question was dormant but recent events in these days brought it back to life. The Turks have abolished the state of the Ottomans and built from its remains a republican state in a new form. One of the basic principles of this state is that no individual, whether named Caliph or Sultan, will hold sway in the new government. They also separated religion from the state completely. They nevertheless named one of the former ruling family a Sultan and declared him a spiritual Caliph to all the Muslims.[97]

These events, Rashid Ridha contends, made it imperative for him to explain the rules of the Shari'a in detail regarding the whole question, and to discuss 'the place of the Caliphate as a system of government among other systems and its history and what should be done in this day and age'.[98]

His contribution to the debate consists of three major parts. The first deals with the theories and ideas of earlier scholars such as Mawardi and Taftazani.[99] The second part consists of a historical exposition from the point of view of

Rashid Ridha of the operation of the Caliphate in history. The third consists of his advice to the Muslim community, especially the Turks, concerning the restoration of the true Caliphate. In the analysis that follows, our interest will naturally concentrate on Ridha's own ideas, both as regarding the history of the Caliphate and his suggestions concerning its restoration.

Rashid Ridha approaches this problem in the manner not of the political scientist but of the theologian. The ideal period of the Caliphate is that of the four rightly guided Caliphs. These are the Caliphs who followed strictly the Sunna of the Prophet, and because of this the religion of Islam spread and its power grew. The institution of Caliphate, Rashid Ridha believes, was a new experience in human history. Prior to the coming of the Prophet Muhammad people suffered under the tyranny of their rulers. Except in a few instances, injustice, severity and deprivation was the lot of the ruled. But the Prophet 'came with the message bringing worldly reform and religious guidance'. One of the basic principles of this guidance was that he established for mankind a middle way religion, a just law and a consultative state; made their affairs the subject of consultation amongst them and abolished the autocracy of kings, their selfishness and conceit. He decreed that the head of their state, the symbol of their unity whose responsibility is to make organisation and justice uniform in the nation, be chosen by election. The electors are the leaders of opinion, respectability (*adalah*) and knowledge, who are trusted by the nation, and he made the head of state responsible to them and equal in the eyes of the law to the lowest man in the land. He enjoined them to obey the head of the state in what is known to be truth and justice and forbade them to obey him in what is sinful, transgressible or unjust. He placed the motive force in performing all this in our religion to ensure compliance both in secret and in public for the 'true obedience is to Allah alone'.[100] Rashid Ridha was not simply reporting the law in its ideal sense but he was suggesting that it was actually complied with and followed, that the system as depicted in the above passage was meant to be universal as Islam is.

He was aware that with the exception of the first Caliph the other three were assassinated, a situation that could not possibly be considered ideal; but he found a ready explanation in attributing blameworthy developments to foreign elements. The murder of 'Umar 'did not result from envy or hatred on the part of the Muslims, not from the ambition of a possible successor but from the secret society of Majus who killed him in revenge for the conquest of their country'.[101] The murder of 'Uthman was no less easy to explain but this time it was not the Persians alone who engineered the conspiracy; a Jew by the name of Abd Allah Ibn Saba' propagated some destructive doctrines amongst Muslims which ended in the rebellion against 'Uthman. The murder of 'Ali and the first civil war were only consequences of these foreign activities. Here, therefore, is an ideal society and an ideal government and an ideal faith which were divested of their deserved success by the encroachment of the foreign elements.

Mu'awiyah completed the process when he captured government by force of arms and established a monarchy. He failed to follow the path of the Rashidun and the guidance of the Qur'an and the Sunna of the Prophet. If it had not been for this failure, the Caliphate would not have attracted those slaves of pleasure and fame for 'There is no bodily pleasure in the office of Caliphate nor is there an autocratic authority.'[102]

He attributes this trend to the expansion of Muslim domain, the accumulation of many enemies to Islam from amongst the leaders of religions or nations that were conquered by Islam. Added to this external factor, Rashid Ridha identifies an internal one present in non-Arabs who adopted Islam and also those Arabs, other than the early Muslims, whose adherence to Islam was not strong, as they have not understood it completely.

> The difficulty in communication made it easy for the Sab'is and the Majus to spread disorder for Islam and the Arabs. It made it also easier for Mu'awiyah to build up an army to fight the true Imam and to make the Caliphate a monarchy.[103]

For Rashid Ridha the struggle was between two ethical systems: the just (Islamic) one and the unjust which sprang from quarters bent on enmity to Islam. Those members of the Muslim community who were incapable of understanding the faith and who therefore did not experience the moral compulsion to follow its tenets were a ready prey for the enemy.

Ridha continues his moralistic analysis of the historical development of the *Ummah*, attributing all its ills to foreign influences. The final decline of the Abbasids, for instance, is attributed by him to the flattery of the Turkish soldiers who, being unfamiliar with Islam and foreign to the egalitarian sentiments of the Arabs, treated the Caliphs like Gods and in the processs divested them of all the vestiges of power.[104]

At this stage, he contends, it was impossible to sustain a system of government in accordance with the Rashidun tradition, or the way of the Umayyads, or early Abbasids who, as he now suggests, combined 'worldly glory with religious interests'.[105] By the time it was possible to effect the form that the Muslim government should take, the power of religion itself had declined and with it the whole civilisation of Islam. In consequence, the Muslims 'were not as successful as were the Franks [Europeans] in abolishing the autocracy of kings'.[106]

But how could the Europeans without the benefit of the true religion outstrip the Muslims? Ridha assures us that there are elements of true Christianity in the West which sustain its civilisation.[107] These elements were, however, soon disappearing heralding the decline of Europe. The Muslims, on the other hand, have broken God's covenant and therefore have been punished.[108]

Ridha emphasises the religious foundation of the political system of the *Ummah* and discounts 'Asabiyyah as the basis of Muslim government in early times. This is in contradiction to Ibn Khaldun's analysis of the rise to power and its later loss by Quraish. Perhaps in the whole work nothing demonstrates the limitations of Rashid Ridha better than his discussion of Ibn Khaldun's theory. He is obviously appalled at such a mundane explanation which reduced the charismatic community to the same level as other human communities. Rashid Ridha, who in other contexts accepts the 'laws of society' as he conceives them to be neutral with regard to religion, insists in this context that Islam has made the Arabs different so that they lost their 'Asabiyyah and consequently were defeated by the Persians.[109] Such an interpretation of history hardly accords with the evidence.

His proposals, which were addressed to the Turks, advised them to call in a representative assembly elected freely by the people to take over from the military authorities. As for the question of the Caliphate, he suggested that it should be left to the Muslim peoples and the independent and semi-independent Muslim governments. He appeals to the Turks to save the world from 'Muslim ignorance and European materialism'[110] by establishing the divine law and the Caliphate of Islam.

Like 'Abduh, Ridha regards the Caliph as the head of the community in the temporal as well as the religious sense. His spiritual power, however, encompassed all Muslims, including those who do not come under his rule.[111]

The large majority of Muslims agree that the establishment of the Caliphate is obligatory on the *Ummah*. Most authorities before Rashid Ridha were content to enumerate as evidence the practices of the Companions and the fact that it was regarded as essential to the proper performance of Muslim duties. Rashid Ridha, as is his habit, resorts to the Tradition for further evidence.[112]

But who shall establish the Caliph? Rashid Ridha, following the Sunni position, makes it the function of the 'Ahl Al Hal Wa Al 'Aqd' (the people who are able to loosen and bind). But who are these people? Do they have to agree unanimously or would a majority suffice? Leaving aside the niceties of majority versus unanimity within this authoritative group, we must concentrate our attention on finding who they are, how they are formed, the basis of their authority and the limits of their power. Rashid Ridha, quoting from 'Abduh, deals with this question more extensively in the Tafsir of the verse calling on Muslims to obey 'Allah, his Messenger and Ulu Al-Amr'. He defines the *Ulu Al-Amr* in this fashion: 'Ulu Al-Amr in every community, county or tribe are known. They are those whom the people trust in the affairs of worldly and religious nature because they believe them to be better informed and more sincere in their advice.'[113] He suggests that they were with the Prophet wherever he went but they dispersed after the conquests of various regions in the Muslim Empire. He also states that when the Muslims wanted to install a new Caliph they sent to the generals and leaders of the people in the various countries to obtain their allegiance (Bay'a).

There is no adequate definition in all this. We are not told clearly who these authoritative people are, or how they emerged and operated in history. One must suspect that the concept of *Ulu Al-Amr* is a question of dogma rather than history. They appear to have disappeared or at least to have been deprived of their rightful position by the emergence of the Umayyads. The Abbasids did nothing to restore their position, nor did the Turks in the successor states. All these governments were not based in the opinion of Ridha on obedience to Allah, his Messenger and *Ulu Al-Amr*. Rashid Ridha, however, seeks to help by giving a definition of the *Ulu Al-Amr* in his day and age. He says that:

> They are the leaders of the *ulema*, the chiefs of the armed forces, the judges and the big merchants, agriculturalists and those concerned with public affairs, the directors of societies and companies, the leaders of political parties, the important writers, doctors and lawyers, providing they are trusted by the nation in its affairs.[114]

Rashid Ridha, feeling that his definition was inadequate as it does not give any clear claim to membership to any person of the categories he mentions, resorts to the simple, if not simple-minded, device of suggesting that these leaders of opinion are known in every country and it would be easy for the head of the government to identify them and to gather them for the purpose of consultation.[115] He thus falls back on the moralist concept of the good ruler who will call in the *Ulu Al-Amr* simply because of their moral excellence.

This obscure group with its obscure basis in society and

equally obscure powers *vis-à-vis* the executive was, however, treated by Rashid Ridha as the final authority in the affairs of the Muslims. Their advice must be sought by the Caliph and it is they who should establish the Caliphate and dismiss the Caliph if he fails in his duties. These authoritative people are not legislators in the strict sense, they are simply Mujtahids bound by the Shari'a itself.

The role of the general public in the classical theory of the Caliphate, which is followed closely by Rashid Ridha, was, to say the least indirect, if not completely negative. It is true that the *Ulu Al-Amr* were defined as those who are able to command the following of the *Ummah*. But the means for this are not clearly stated. The army commanders surely are seldom followed for other reasons than the military force behind them. The *ulema,* the lawyers, the merchants and all the other categories must in the end rely on the same basis. The history of Islam itself shows that the armed forces superseded all other authorities and institutions. Rashid Ridha was aware of this fact, but his adherence to the classical theory in its totality prevented him from offering any proper remedies beyond the hope that the generals will be such pious men that their authority and power will not be used illegally.

This confusion regarding the *Ulu Al-Amr* bedevils all Ridha's efforts in formulating a consistent and tangible theory. His grafting of some Western institutions such as a house of representatives (to which reference will be made presently) helps to increase the confusion; for unlike the legislature in European societies, the house of assembly in Rashid Ridha's concept does not legislate but simply seeks to discover the law of God. There are, of course, parallels, although on a limited scale, in European societies. The House of Commons in Britain does not often go against the tenets of the Church in social matters such as marriage and divorce. But this is so because of deference to public opinion and not because the House by the very nature of its establishment is limited by these religious laws. Whatever the state of public opinion might be in a Muslim society, Rashid Ridha would not wish the *Ulu Al-Amr* to follow unless it conforms with the tenets of Muslim law. The supposed representatives of the people are therefore a committee of Muslim jurists engaged in classical Shari'a discussion. They are not to divide for voting. Any difference must be referred to the specialists for advice. Since the concern is for the truth rather than the trend of opinion of the people, majority vote is irrelevant.[116]

The leaders of opinion whose categories he mentions pre-suppose a free society. They cannot, as he admits, emerge or function under conditions of autocratic rule whether by foreign or native administration. Dictatorship of whatever variety deprives the nation of its natural leaders either through corruption or removal by force.[117]

He observes that the Egyptians and Turks are striving to form parliaments. He declares these parliaments to be 'in essence the same as the *Ahl Al-Hal Wa Al-'Aqd* in Islam, except that Islam requires them to be people of knowledge and moral excellence which neither the Europeans nor their imitators demand.'[118] Once more he does not feel inclined to subscribe to the concept of a general suffrage as the Westernisers were advocating. Inherent in the whole concept is the limitation imposed on the political behaviour of the religious society by the fact of it being religious. The person or persons to be elected as representatives of the Muslim community must first pass the test of religious knowledge and conformity to religious morals.[119] This is inevitable, just as in the case of certain states where an elected member must not violate the political principles of the state. The identity of the state and religion in Muslim political theory makes the position completely logical and arguments against it are in essence arguments against the concept of this identity.

Since the historical development of the last few centuries deprived the *Ummah* of its proper leaders, and since without them no normal political life is possible, what then is the course of action? Rashid Ridha asks himself this question:

Is there anyone in the Muslim countries of the *Ahl Ah-Hal Wa Al-Aqd* who is able to undertake this cause [the Caliphate] and if there is not anybody with actual in-fluence, are there some who are potentially influential? And if so, is it not possible for the Muslims to establish a system to make this potential influence an actual one?

He answers this positively, admitting that the task is hard but it required a strong advocate. He pins his hopes on the moderate reformist Islamic Party, namely his own. The party he conceives as the one standing in the middle of two extremes: the rigid imitators of the *fiqh'* books and the equally slavish imitators of western ideas. This moderate party of his

> combined independence in understanding Islam and the rules of the Shari'a and the essence of European civilisation. This party is the only one able to abolish disunity within the *Ummah* on the questions of what is to be done to revive the Caliphate.[120]

Rashid Ridha was not oblivious of the fact of the strong penetration of European ideas such as nationalism with all its implications of secularism into the deepest areas of Muslim thought. He was one of the earliest thinkers to recognise the dangers of nationalism although he may have supported its final goal, of freedom from colonial domination. Various nationalisms emerging in the Muslim world acted on the unity of Islam, seeking to replace its universal ideology by a parochial one. The dismembering of the *Umma* in this 'fashion would militate against the revival of the Caliphate, for in the eyes of Rashid Ridha only one Caliphate was possible and legitimate.[121]

The obstacles in the face of reviving the true Caliphate were not only in the absence of the *Ahl Al-Hal Wa Al-'Aqd* but also in the absence of candidates for the high office who could meet the stiff conditions formulated by traditional theory. Among these conditons they mention such knowledge of Islam as to permit for independent thought (Ijtihad) and apart from personal excellence, moral and physical courage, genealogical purity must also obtain. The candidate must belong to the tribe of Quraish.[122] Rashid Ridha was insistent on the Quraishi condition but not, he wishes to assure us, because of any consideration except compliance with the authentic Tradition and the consensus of the Companions. He branded Abu Al-Kalam Azad's egalitarian ideas as violating these Traditions, although Azad utilised precisely the same technique as did Ridha regarding the question of apostasy. As the candidates from Quraish who met all the conditions were obviously few, limiting the choice of the *Ummah*, Rashid Ridha hit on the idea of establishing a school for the candidates to the Caliphate.[123] Rashid Ridha was incapable of understanding the egalitarian nature of the forces of nationalism and the need to give an equally egalitarian interpretation to Islam. The claim of Quraish, however, justified in religious texts and Muslim past history could no longer be taken seriously in the modern world. Indeed, if anything the restricted concept of the Imamate prevalent among the Shi'a may be more logical than the half-way house position of the Sunnis. Rashid Ridha himself subscribed to this idea, but on the grounds of the certainty of the descent of the Hashemis.

Rashid Ridha having decided that the Caliphate must be Arab and must have as its occupant a Mujtahid, he went on to the local conclusion of declaring Arabic a national language for all Muslims. He was, however, equivocal about it. He says,

It is not our intention to call upon all the non-Arab Muslims to learn Arabic. We simply remind the reformist party of what is known to most of its members, that is the strong connection between the office of the Caliph and the Arabic language.

He further claims that 'It is impossible for the Muslims to be acquainted with each other and to be united to the best degree possible without Arabic.'[124]

The end of Rashid Ridha's proposals was to resurrect the Arab Caliphate. His motives were a combination of the attraction of early Islam in its Arab purity, a revulsion from innovations and decadence associated with the coming of the non-Arabs and their machinations. The veneer of European institutions appeared to cause more confusion in Ridha's political concepts than clarification.[125] He suffers, like the early jurists, from great reliance on persons, not institutions.

The central difficulty in the classical theory of the Caliphate stems from the lack of specific description of those powers of the *Ummah* relating to the choice of the Caliph. Ridha does not give any clarification of the problem. The terms *Ahl Al-Hal Wa Al-'Aqd* (those who are able to loosen and bind), the *Ulu Al-Amr* (those in authority), the *Ahl Al-Shura* (those who are to be consulted by the ruler), the *Ahl Al-Ijma'* (those who are legally authoritative and whose consensus is binding), were never accorded clear social definitions through which they could be identified. The *Jam'a* or *Ummah* (the community of believers) was not given free choice of its supposed members of parliament. Ridha, following 'Abduh, insisted that election to parliament must be free from compulsion, that the nation must select its *Ahl Al-Hal Wa Al-'Aqd* without interference from the executive. Such a sentiment deserves our respect and sympathy, particularly since the experience of Egypt under Isma'il showed how ineffectual the consultative committee were *vis-à-vis* the pressure of the ruler. This, however, is not extended to allowing the common people to learn from their mistakes. Ridha insists that the *Ummah* should be free to choose providing that it chooses the right people. If it failed to do so, it would be automatically disqualified.[126] Yet Ridha does not give the public any means of identifying the leaders it must choose. He uses circular definitions that are most unhelpful and sometimes suggests that they are known to everybody, and the ruler if he so wishes could consult them.[127] It is, therefore, essential to realise that the Western terms used by Rashid Ridha are not necessarily employed in the same way as in the Western context.

Perhaps the best assessment of his efforts in political thought is that of Emile Tyan, who commenting on H. Laoust's translation of 'Al Khilafa' under the title 'Le califat dans la doctrine de Rasid Rida' by declaring that Ridha could hardly be credited with having a special doctrine on this matter. 'All the personal efforts of this author, animated by a very intense religious and apologetic spirit led him to propose certain adaptations in order to make possible the restoration of the Caliphate in modern Muslim states.'[128] A similar view is expressed by Louis Gardet, who credits Rashid Ridha with having recast Western assumptions in a Muslim fashion.[129]

We must, however, realise that despite Ridha's wish and hope to restore the Caliphate, he, unlike Al Mawardi, was less preoccupied with the legitimisation and regularisation of the institutions in being, and more with outlining the ideal political organisation.[130]

There is an important point in Ridha's exposition of the Islamic political system, namely the question of minorities. He advises the non-Muslims in Muslim domains to trust their future to a Caliphal government, which would given them autonomy, in preference to a secular one, which would deprive them of it. Further, the Muslim government is tied with the moral law of Islam which does not bind the civilian politicians.[131] There is nothing in all this about the participation in government by non-Muslims; but in 1909 Ridha wrote in support of the régime of the Society of Unity and Progress that 'consultation between Muslims and non-Muslims and sharing each other's opinions is not prohibited. It may even be obligatory.'[132] He therefore saw no reason to question the membership of non-Muslims in the parliament, especially when they are not dominant in number over the Muslims.

Rashid Ridha's Impact on Egyptian and Muslim Thought

Al Manar, Rashid Ridha's main contribution to modern Muslim journalism, was by far the most successful of its kind and the most influential. It was due in large measure to the personality of Rashid Ridha and his extensive contacts throughout the Muslim world that it was read in Java as well as in Morocco and that its influence was felt in Zanzibar and Mombasa as in Muslim Russia. Correspondents from all over the world kept in contact with him and he sent complimentary copies of *Al Manar* to various Muslim organisations and leaders. He utilised the journal to project the personality of 'Abduh as the leader of a reform party throughout the Muslim world.[133] It is a measure of Rashid Ridha's success that 'Abduh's name became known throughout the lands of Islam.

After the death of 'Abduh, Rashid Ridha assumed the leadership of the Salafi movement. Through *Al Manar*,

Rashid Ridha's leadership was not in dispute; but even if it had not existed, Ridha's powerful personality, extensive learning and his success in maintaining and exploiting contacts would have brought him the leadership of the Manarists.

Events in Egypt and the Muslim world isolated him somewhat from the main stream of Muslim thought. The task that he and 'Abduh set for themselves was difficult. It was more so for Rashid Ridha, who was hardly touched by European culture. The pace of Westernisation in Egypt attracted the bulk of 'Al Imam's Party' while the hostility of the conservatives to Rashid Ridha was intensified after the death of his teacher and protector. Rashid Ridha's ventures into Egyptian and Turkish politics brought him few friends. The rise of nationalism in Egypt isolated him still further for he objected to the movement naturally as a Syrian, but more so as a Muslim. He saw the nationalism of Egypt and other Muslim countries as a foreign incursion leading to the fragmentation of the *Ummah* and the further weakening of Islam.[134] Though in the long run this may in fact have been true, the nationalism of Egypt, or at least the nationalism of the Mustafa Kamil party, was vastly different in the sense that it had a place in it for Islam. As Rashid Ridha well knew, the party was regarded as a Muslim party,[135] but it was Rashid Ridha's need or his conviction to keep friendly, or as friendly as possible, with the British administration that brought him the enmity of the party even when the effective leadership passed over to the religiously oriented Abd Al-Aziz Jawish.

His idealisation of 'Abduh and Al-Afghani hampered to some degree any objective study of either. He treated their lives and works almost as he treated religious texts. The reader could not help sometimes being overwhelmed by the personalities of two men who at his hands were turned into less of historical figures and more of legends. He saw in front of his eyes what the conservatives had warned of all along, namely the growth of Westernisation in Egypt and faced the accusation that 'Abduh and himself were responsible for its growth. His defence that Westernisation predated the reformist party was essentially true, but irrelevant to the substance of the accusation. There is no doubt that the Salafi weakened the authority of the traditional *ulema* and that 'Abduh in his later life allied himself with those who were more oriented towards Europe and who later proved to be much closer to the Westernisers. Thus, Rashid Ridha gained 'Abduh's enemies and lost most of his friends.

Undercurrents were moving steadily in opposite directions from the secularisation of Egyptian life. The virtual disappearance of the Nationalist Party and the domination of the strongly nationalistic Wafd of Egyptian politics created a gap between the nation and its leaders. This gap was hidden behind the smoke of emotion aroused in the heady years after the First World War and the turbulence of the early twenties. As the dust settled down and Egypt began to fall into the pattern of political musical chairs, which lasted until 1952,[136] the gap between the political leaders and their Western ideas on the one hand and the common people inspired by Islamic ideas and tradition was growing wider. Within this gap stepped Rashid Ridha and many of his friends. At this level he was willing to co-operate with the reactionary *ulema* of Al Azhar. It was not by accident that religious societies such as the Young Men's Muslim Association,[137] and the Muslim Brotherhood made their first appearance during this period and both had certain connections with Rashid Ridha. In spite of his quarrel with Al Azhar he moved perceptibly towards reconciliation, providing in all circumstances that no one should do violence to any of his principal beliefs.

In the field of thought proper his tremendous energy and powerful pen which were previously preoccupied with the *ulema* became more and more involved in arguments with the other extreme of the trilogy. The middle position which Rashid Ridha sought to occupy dictates that the greatest resistance must be directed at the side which exerts the greatest pull. At the turn of the century it was the *ulema* of Al Azhar who held sway but within twenty years the picture had completely changed and the Westernisers represented the greatest danger. If Rashid Ridha's advice to the *ulema* was liberalism, his advice to the Westernisers was restraint. He led the attacks on Ali Abd Al-Raziq for his now famous book on the Caliphate,[138] and was delighted when the authorities of Al Azhar punished the author with severity. He was also in the forefront of the critics of Taha Hussain's theory on pre-Islamic poetry and found himself in this respect at variance with Lutfi Al-Sayyid, who early in the century was regarded by him as a prominent member of 'Al Imam's Party'. Both Abd Al-Raziq and Taha Hussain were phenomena of an Egypt exposed to a greater degree of Westernisation than Ridha would have liked.

The arguments against these writers were conducted by *ulema* not always with identical views to those of Ridha. But the authorities and not the writers in the end decided how the argument should be settled. Both Abd Al-Raziq and Taha Hussain lost their posts and the latter was forced to alter the offending section of his book. But neither was argued completely out of court; they both became symbols of a secularist and liberal ideology. The opposition to them took the form of traditionalism. In this issue there did not appear to be a middle course.

The early followers of 'Abduh from the Western-educated were quickly disappearing. Their whole educational system and the changed conditions of Egypt reduced the religious argument from a position of importance in educated circles, replacing it with questions of politics and nationalist appeal. Religion was gradually relegated to a secondary place as a mere individual relationship between the citizen and the deity he elects to worship. The *Ummah* appeared to have chosen the security of unity with non-Muslims in Egypt in preference to the romantic affiliation with Muslims outside. It was Al Azhar and institutions built around it such as Dar-Al-Ulum that put a certain degree of restraint. Al Azhar did not stand against nationalism but it did not subscribe to isolationism. It must have been strange for Rashid Ridha to realise that only within Al Azhar and the circles of the Nationalist Party would he find his allies. The changes imposed on the curricula of Al Azhar and the growth of knowledge amongst its younger *ulema* prepared a climate of opinion to make it more open to new ideas. Rashid Ridha, on the other hand, was perceptibly retreating from the adventurous position of the early years of the century. The grounds for co-operation were thus present, but Ridha had a merciless pen and a tendency to criticise immoderately. This did not endear him to the Azharites of his day. In the event, therefore, 'Abduh was gradually being accepted while Rashid Ridha was being simply ignored. Ridha's heirs were to be found later within the circles of the Muslim Brothers, the Young Men's Muslim Association and similar organisations.

The growth of these movements in Egypt was a reaction to extreme Westernisation. It was to such a powerful reaction that avowed Westernisers such as Haykal, Taha Hussain and Tawfik Al-Hakim had to respond by modifying their position of extreme secularism and speaking or writing in more glowing tones about Islam.[139] How much of this reaction could be attributed at least in part to Rashid Ridha is difficult to ascertain. His persistence and tenacity, his unlimited self-confidence and evident contempt for Westernisers, however high their position in society or government, must have contributed to stimulating that reaction. Further, Rashid Ridha's stand on classical Islam and his conviction that it could withstand all arguments against it must be regarded as one of the foundations of the movements later to become so powerful in Egyptian society.

Outside Egypt Rashid Ridha, like Muhammad 'Abduh, was held in greater esteem. Many imitators of *Al Manar* emerged in many parts of the Muslim world, and in Malaya in particular a group of Malay Arabs translated selected articles from it and published them in the journal *Al-Imam*. The magazine was also widely read and imitated in Sumatra, and it influenced the Muhammadiyyah movement in Java. The convulsion of the Muslim world in the decades after his death brought into focus his ideas and those of his earlier masters.

Rashid Ridha as a Thinker

Compared with Al-Afghani and 'Abduh, Rashid Ridha was the least acquainted with Western thought.[140] He learned no foreign language and his knowledge of Western ideas were of second- or even third-hand nature. But of the three he was perhaps the best trained, and certainly the most knowledgeable in the field of Tradition. His mind could not tolerate ambiguity and, unlike 'Abduh, he could not stand happily with two contradictory ideas pretending that both could be held without difficulty. He lacked 'Abduh's polish and sophistication and had to contend with more acute problems than he did. His facade of liberalism or tolerance within the *Ummah* in the interest of unity did not prevent him from lashing out at any opponent if he felt incensed. Although he agreed with the theoretical position of 'Abduh, he applied it much more strictly and therefore much more narrowly. The role of reason in his view was to rebel against the authority of the traditional *ulema* and their masters on the one hand, and against blind Westernisation on the other. In relation to revelation, however, the position of reason in Rashid Ridha's system appeared less free than in 'Abduh's. While 'Abduh may suggest that the story of Adam and Hawa' is allegorical, referring to the stages of man's development, Ridha refrains from tampering with the revelation in this way.[141]

Like 'Abduh, Rashid Ridha was more concerned with the didactic rather than the philosophical. In fact he measures the efforts of the early scholars from precisely this point of view. Although he may use the word philosopher to prefix the name of Al-Afghani or 'Abduh, this is no indication of his appreciation of Muslim philosophy. Hostility to philosophy and Sufism is inherent in the school of Ibn Taimiya of which Rashid Ridha was an exponent. (In over thirty years of publication *Al Manar* has published not one considerable work by a Muslim philosopher.) Philosophical complexities were rejected out of hand as a deviation from revelation and as didactically harmful. Islam, in the view of Rashid Ridha, did not need a new philosophy as much as it needed a simple exposition to make it within reach of the average person.

His attitude to science was vastly different from his attitude towards philosophy. Here the impressive achievements of the scientists have conferrred an aura on the sciences as disciplines and also on scientific theories that no philosopher could aspire to. The school of Al-Afghani was primarily concerned with interpreting Islam in scientifically accepted terms and it appears that all of them have raised the status of theory to the level of fact. It was probably this particular attitude which prompted both 'Abduh and Rashid Ridha to seek to reduce the miraculous elements in the Qur'an to a minimum. Although Rashid Ridha might support 'Abduh's position on some of these questions he would be more inclined to subscribe to the old Salafi doctrine of accepting the texts with the proviso of 'Bila Kaif'.[142]

In 'Abduh's system public morality was partially freed from its religious basis and Rashid Ridha, while theoretically approving 'Abduh's position, retreated from it in practice. This difference may be attributed to Ridha's greater knowledge of the Tradition and less acquaintance with other cultures. He, however, maintained that differences in matters of details or indeed in a question of doctrine should be tolerated within the Muslim community in the interest of unity. This attitude was dictated by the wider social and political considerations rather than the strictly intellectual appreciation of opposite views.[143]

Rashid Ridha was a revivalist preoccupied with the preaching of the doctrines of Islam in a simple and more acceptable form. Like all theologians, he conceived the role of reason to be the elaboration and elucidation of revelation. Like the jurists he regarded his task as discovering from the texts the appropriate rules for pious life. In his system, philosophy has no role and science as an undeniable fact helps in the process of interpreting hidden meanings of the Qur'an and the Tradition. Though he owes his thought to Ghazali and Ibn Taimiya, he subordinates the former to the latter and sees Al Ghazali, as he does all the figures he admires, to have ended his life as a Salafi.[144]

Reform, as seen by Al-Afghani and more so by 'Abduh, consisted of balancing two elements, the irreducible and unchanging aspects of Islam and the need to change in other aspects to meet modern conditions.[145] The equilibrium between the two elements was upset in favour of the former by Ridha and if later leaders such as Al-Banna attacked the West and rejected it as a model this must be regarded as at least partially inspired by this trend.

Al Afghani, Muhammad 'Abduh and Rashid Ridha

The journey of reformist Islam covering over half a century shows the stages of its growth and development. Al-Afghani injected a sense of urgency and a liberal ideology, while 'Abduh sought to demonstrate the congruity of Islam and modernity. The first was content with general proposals. The second formulated a more detailed proposal but found it essential to limit the role of human thought to the simple activity of removing apparent contradiction within revelation or between a revelation and what was regarded as science. Internal consistency was thus achieved sometimes at the expense of external realities. Rashid Ridha demonstrated still further this departure from reality, and together with greater internal coherence. The basic question of the relevance of Islam to Egyptian society both as a legal system and religious outlook was touched only in apologetic fashion. Despite liberalism in legal matters none of the leaders of reformist Islam was willing to allow fundamental alteration of the law. On the theological plane their most significant contributions appeared in arguments with European orientalists.[146] Rashid Ridha's lamentation that many Muslims read with delight the powerful rejoinder of 'Abduh to Hanotaux without concern about its contents[147] may have stemmed from the actual irrelevance of the whole affair to the true needs of Muslim society.

The reformist school, like the conservative *ulema*, was overtaken by developments in Egyptian and modern society. Both grew more and more irrelevant to its basic spiritual and social problems. Nevertheless the appeal of Islam remains powerful and the social, political and economic transformation had to be legitimised in the eyes of Islam to be acceptable with a clear conscience by the ordinary Muslim. This task of piecemeal admittance of change lacks cohesion or systematic examination of the facts and in consequence the *ulema* have taken a back seat in these matters, resorting as their conservative predecessors did to issuing Fatwas in accordance with the wishes of the political power.

The task of the *ulema* has ceased to be the discovery of the revealed law and has become more openly and frankly

the support of 'the necessary changes'. In short, the reformist
Muslim thinker of our day can no longer offer the lead. He
must simply follow. This was inherent though not immediately obvious in the reformist approach. Rashid Ridha, as
previously noted, once suggested that all the necessary
laws of modern civilisation could be accommodated within
the framework of the Shari'a with the exception of a few
rules concerning Riba.

Reformist Islam consequently was incapable of leadership.
The way was left wide open to another reaction to the impact of modernity, the revolutionary reaction. Where intellectual argument is not a satisfying exercise, forceful action is
bound to be. This type of reaction does not call for the few
to charter the way, but for the many to make one.

NOTES

CHAPTER 1

1. E. G. Browne, *The Persian Revolution of 1905-1909* (Cambridge, 1910) portrays Al-Afghani as a hero of the revolution; and B. Michel and Shaikh Moustafha Abdal Razik, *Cheikh Mohammed Abdou, Rissalat al-Tawhid Expose de la Religion Musulmane* (Paris, 1925) say in the introduction (p. 23), 'Wherever he went he left behind a turbulent revolution. It is no exaggeration to state that all the nationalist liberation movements and the movements against European designs which we have witnessed in the East go back directly to his agitation.' W. S. Blunt, *Secret History of the English Occupation of Egypt* (New York, 1922) describes him as 'the true originator of the liberal religious reform' (p. 76).

2. Muhammad Al-Makhzumi, *Khatirat Jamal Al Din Al-Afghani* (Beirut, 1931) reports Al-Afghani as saying that Lord Salisbury offered him the throne of the Sudan in exchange for his co-operation in its conquest, but Al-Afghani refused. See p. 54.

3. Elie Kedourie, 'Nouvelle Lumiere sur Afghani et 'Abduh', Orient, no. 30, 1964, pp. 37-55 and no. 31, 1964, pp. 83-104, argues that the reputation of both Al-Afghani and 'Abduh was posthumous and questions a great many of Al-Afghani's claims.

4. Muhammad Rashid Ridha, *Tarikh Al Ustaz Al Imam Al Shaikh Muhammad 'Abduh*, vol. I (Cairo, 1st ed., 1931), p. 25.

5. Ibid., p. 30.

6. *Tarikh*, vol. II, p. 45 and Ibrahim 'Abduh, *A'laam Al-Sahafa Al-Arabiyya* (Cairo, 2nd ed., 1948), p. 117.

7. Cf. Nadav Safran, *Egypt in Search of Political Community* (London, 1961), pp. 47 ff. and Mahmoud Al Khafif, *Ahmad 'Urabi* (Cairo, 1947), pp. 26-7.

8. *Khatirat*, p. 35.

9. *Tarikh*, vol. II (Cairo, 2nd ed., 1344 A.H.), p. 7. 'Abduh mentions in an article published in about the second half of 1879 that Al-Afghani 'resumed teaching after an interval of more than one year'.

10. *Tarikh*, vol. I, pp. 46-7. 'Amhouri reports the increased activities of Al-Afghani in the political field in 1878 through the use of his pen and those of his friends, and that he 'began to mix with the mass of the people' to arouse them against the government. Quotation from p. 47

11. Al-Afghani's contribution to the magazine *Misr* about absolute government *'al-hukumat al-istibdadiyyah'* (republished in *Al Manar*, vol. III, pp. 577-82 and 601-7) and also his article on the 'True Cause for the Happiness of Man' (*Al-'illat al-Hagigiyyat li Sa'adat al Insan*) republished in *Al Manar*, vol. XXIII, pp. 37-45, contained nothing which indicated allegiance to a specific religion. Also the contributions of his disciple 'Abduh collected in Rashid Ridha's *Tarikh*, vol. II (2nd ed.), pp. 2-48, hardly refers to religion as such, except in one article, pp. 37-45, calling upon the *ulema* to allow the study of modern sciences. In a particular article 'Abduh, no doubt under the influence of Al-Afghani, decries religious differences in favour of unity for the defence of the motherland, p. 35.

12. *Tarikh*, vol. I, p. 41. Adib Ishaq reports that Al-Afghani 'harboured a great hatred for the English state'. He also reports him as having met with the French Consul General (c. 1879), no doubt to enlist his support.

13. *Khatirat*, pp. 223-4.

14. Ibid., p. 35.

15. Ibid., p. 46.

16. *Al Manar*, vol. III, pp. 606-7.

17. Ibid., p. 577.

18. *Khatirat*, p. 90.

19. *Al Manar*, vol. XXIII, p. 39. and *Tarikh*, vol. I p. 47. He called on Egyptians to stand as Egyptians distinct from all other Muslims, Turkish or Arab.

20. Blunt, *Secret History*, pp. 95 and 101 refers to a conspiracy by Al-Afghani to assassinate Isma'il in 1879, and *Tarikh*, vol. II (2nd ed.), pp. 335-6.

21. Mahmoud Al-Khafif, op. cit., p. 82, describes the scene when 'Urabi confronted the Khedive with these words.

22. Cf. Shakib Arslan, *Hadhir al-'alam al-Islami* (Cairo, 1352 A.H.), vol. II, p. 292.

23. *Tarikh*, vol. I, p. 6, introduction, reports Al-Afghani as saying to a Tartar student of his, 'Son, you will perform the funeral prayer on Czardom and you will attend the funeral of British power in India.'

24. *Al 'Urwat Al Wuthqa* (Cairo, 1957) p. 96. Al-Afghani accused Ahmad Khan of aiming at helping the British through corrupting Muslim beliefs. Quoted by M. Al-Bahay, *Modern Islamic Thought and its Relation with Western Colonialism* (Cairo, 1957), p. 15.

25. *Khatirat*, p. 245.

26. Al-Afghani, *Al Bayan fi Tarikh al Inkelize wa al Afghan* (*The clear account of the history of the English and Afghanistan*) (Alexandria, 1878).

27. Cf. Osman Amin, *Introduction to Al Radd ala al Dahriyyin* (Cairo and Baghdad, 2nd ed.), p. 8.

28. *Khatirat*, p. 349.

29. Ibid., p. 149.

30. Ibid., p. 154 ff.

31. *Al Manar*, vol. XXIII, p. 37 fn. Rashid Ridha says that the articles published by Al-Afghani in the newspaper *Misr* had 'an influence in the British nation to the extent that their newspapers rebutted his arguments and he replied in a way that raised his prestige and this *was the first reason for his name to be known in Europe*' (my italics).

32. Elie Kedourie, op. cit., no. 31, p. 93, where he quotes the Indian CID memorandum which claims that Al-Afghani offered his services to the British government and that his offer was declined. Surely, if he were willing to do so, he could have done so at a later date and with considerable rewards.

33. Rashid Ridha, *Al Manar*, vol. II, p. 245, says that the conservative *ulema* were critical of Al-Afghani on three counts: his knowledge of philosophy, his violation of certain customs which were considered part of the religion and the fact that he was surrounded by many irreligious persons.

34. Perhaps the earliest suspicion of Al-Afghani's conviction based on his statement was that of Mustafa Abd Al-Raziq, *Al Manar*, vol. XXIV, p. 311. Abd Al-Raziq is there reported to have suspected his convictions since his rejoinder to Renan defended the Arabs strongly and Islam in a somewhat lukewarm fashion. Reference was made also to the paragraph where Al-Afghani accepts the contradiction between religion and philosophy. It is the same paragraph which S. G. Haim uses as a central argument for suspecting Al-Afghani's conviction. S. G. Haim, *Arab Nationalism: An Anthology* (Los Angeles, 1962), p. 11.

35. *Tarikh*, vol. I, p. 31.

36. A. M. Goichon, *Réfutation des Matérialistes*, her translation of Al-Afghani's *Al-Radd Ala Al Dahriyyin* (Paris, 1942), Introduction, p. 41, n. 2.

37. Op. cit., p. 50 *et passim*.

38. 'Religion and Irreligion in Iranian Nationalism', *Comparative Studies in Society and History*, vol. IV, pp. 265-95. Quoted by Elie Kedourie, op. cit., no. 30, pp. 38-9.

39. 'Symbol and Sincerity in Islam', *Studia Islamica*, vol. XIX, p. 34, n.2.

40. Op. cit., pp. 122-3.

41. *Al Manar*, vol. XXXIII, pp. 232-3 reports Al-Afghani and 'Abduh wading through the mud at Alexandria to rescue a Muslim youth who had been converted to Christianity by the missionaries. Al-Afghani, remarking on the unconcern shown by Egyptian authorities about the matter, said to 'Abduh, 'It seems we are the only Muslims in this country.'

42. See, for instance, *Al Manar*, vol. XXIV, p. 312, where Rashid Ridha suggests that Al-Afghani's *article* rejoinder to Renan was incorrectly translated.

43. E. Renan, *Histoire générale et système comparé des langues sémitiques* (Paris, 1883), vol. I, 6th ed., pp. 4-5, as quoted by Ibrahim Madkour, *Fi al-Falsafat al-Islamiyyuh* (Cairo, 1947), p. 10.

44. Republished in *Al Manar*, vol. XVI, pp. 44-7.

45. Iraj Afshar and Asghar Mahdavi, *Documents Inédits Concernant Seyyed Jamal al Din Afghani*, Publications de l'Université de Teheran, no. 841, 1963, plate 65. Italics are mine. This letter is not included in Ridha's *Tarikh*, vol. II, which contains 'Abduh's works.

46. Cf. J. Jomier, *Encyclopaedia of Islam*, new ed., p. 419.

47. Cf. Shakib Arslan, *Hadhir al-'Alam al-Islami*, vol. II, p. 301.

48. See Mahmoud Abu Rayyah, *Jamal Al-Din Al-Afghani* (Cairo, no date), p. 156, where the author chides the translators (Sadiq Nash'at and Abd Al Nadim Hasanain) of Mirza Lutfallah Khan's *Jamal Al-Din Al-Asadabadi al Ma 'ruf bi Al-Afghani* (Cairo, 1957) for publishing this book and ends by saying, 'He will remain forever an Afghan, even if they gave us a thousand pieces of evidence.'

49. *Tarikh*, vol. I, p. 33, quotes 'Abduh as saying that Al-Afghani was instructed by *Al 'Urwat Al Wuthqa* Secret Society to publish a journal 'calling upon Muslims to unite under the banner of the Islamic Caliphate'.

50. Ibid., p. 307.

51. Lothrop Stoddard as quoted by Ahmad Amin in *Zu'ama' al-islah* (Cairo, 1948), p. 105, says that Al-Afghani regarded the West as influenced by the spirit of the Crusades and was bent on destroying the Muslim renaissance.

52. Cf. Ahmad Amin. op. cit., p. 113.

53. J. M. Landau, 'Afghani's Pan-Islamic Project', *Islamic Culture*, vol. XXVI, no. 3, p. 50.

54. Cf. Al-Afghani, *Al Qada wal Qadar* (Cairo, no date), pp. 10-11. It is a reprint from *Al'Urwat al Wuthqa* which also appears in *Tarikh*, vol. II, 2nd ed., p. 259.

55. Al-Afghani, *Al Radd 'ala al Dahriyyin*, (Cairo and Baghdad, 2nd ed., 1955), p. 87.

56. Al-Afghani, *Al 'Urwat al Wuthqa* (Cairo, 1957),pp. 70-1.

57. *Al 'Urwat al Wuthqa*, pp. 472-5.

58. Loc. cit. and p. 96.

59. *Tarikh*, vol. I, pp. 82-3 and Abd Al-Qadir Al Maghribi, *Jamal al-Din Al-Afghani* (Cairo, 1948), pp. 95 ff.

60. *Tarikh*, vol. I, loc. cit.

61. Cf. H.A.R. Gibb, *Modern Trends in Islam* (Chicago, 2nd ed., 1950), p. 29.

62. Cf. Abd Al-Qadir al-Maghribi, op. cit., pp. 77 ff.

63. The term reform as used here means placing a greater emphasis on continuity *vis-à-vis* change. Modernisation reverses this formula. Thus the *Salafiyyat* School is reformist, whereas Ahmad Khan and the Secularists are modernists.

64. *Tarikh*, vol. I, p. 82.
65. *Tarikh*, vol. II, pp. 232-3.
66. Loc. cit.
67. *Tarikh*, vol. I, pp. 46-7 and *Zu'ama al Islah*, pp. 72-3.
68. Cf. Aziz Ahmad, 'Ahmad Kahn, Al-Afghani and Muslim India', *Studia Islamica*, vol. XIII, pp. 55-78, especially pp. 56-63.
69. These references are quoted by Muhammed Al-Bahay, op cit., pp. 11-17.
70. Cf. Bashir Ahmad Dar, *Religious Thought of Sayyid Ahmad Khan* (Lahore, 1957), p. 204, quoting Sayyid Muhammad 'Ali.
71. See Al-Ghazali, *Tahafut al-Falasifah*, translated by Sabith Ahmad Kamili (Lahore, 1958), p. 249.
72. *Al Radd*, p. 28.
73. Loc. cit.
74. Ibid., pp. 47-64.
75. Ibid., pp. 77-88.
76. Ibid., p. 86.
77. Ibid., p. 87.
78. See ibid., p. 25 and p. 87.
79. A. Hourani, op. cit., p. 116.
80. *Zu'ama' Al Islah*, p. 113.
81. Loc. cit.
82. Ibid., p. 114 also *Khatirat*, p. 161.
83. *Khatirat*, p. 162.
84. See, for instance, his article quoted by Aziz Ahmad, op cit., p. 59.
85. *Zu'ama Al-Islah*, p. 113.
86. *Al Radd*, p. 80
87. *Tarikh*, vol. I, Introduction, p. n (nun).
88. Al-Afghani's suggestion reported in *Tarikh*, vol. I, p. 33, is highly doubted. He there gives as the reason for suspending the paper, that it no longer reached its public in Egypt and India.
89. *Tarikh*, vol. I, pp. 56-62, contains the letter to Mirza Hassan al-Shirazi, calling upon him to oppose the Shah giving the concession to the British Tobacco Company.
90. According to Al-Afghani, he held 'political offices' in both Persia and Afghanistan. In Egypt he was a teacher though with no specific duties, while in Turkey, according to him, he was offered the office of Shaikh al-Islam.
91. Cf. Aziz Ahmad, op. cit., p. 59 and his *Studies in Islamic Culture* (Clarendon Press, 1964), p. 56.
92. W. C. Smith, *Islam in Modern History* (Princeton, 1957), p. 48.

CHAPTER 2

1. *Tarikh Al Ustaz Al Imam Al Shaikh Muhammad 'Abduh*, vol. I, (Cairo, 1st ed., 1931) p. 289.
2. Ibid., p. 894.
3. Cf. *Tarikh*, vol. I, p. 998, also Shakib Arslan, *'Rashid Ridha aw ikha' arba'ina Sanatan* (Damascus, 1937), pp. 127-8.
4. *Tarikh*, vol. I, p. 974. 'Abduh is there described as more submissive to authority.
5. *Tarikh*, vol. I, p. 974, ff.
6. As quoted in *Tarikh*, vol. I, p. 226.
7. *Tarikh*, vol. II (Cairo 2nd ed., 1344 A. H.) compare his articles on pp. 119 123 and 127 with his articles on pp. 194 and 197.

8. Ibid., p. 538.

9. Ahmad Amin, op. cit., p. 310.

10. His rapid advancement was attributed by some of his contemporary *ulema* to his 'masonic' affiliation, cf. *Al Manar*, vol. VIII, p. 403.

11. Lufti al-Sayyid, *Qessat Hayati* (Cairo, 1962), pp. 58-9.

12. N. Safran, op. cit., p. 273, n.2, holds the opposite view.

13. For the views of Ahmad Khan as compared with Al-Afghani, see Aziz Ahmad, *Studia Islamica*, vol. XIII, pp. 57-78 and the same article in a slightly modified form in *Studies in Islamic Culture in the Indian Environment* by the same author (London, 1964), especially pp. 55-66.

14. C. Adams, *Islam and Modernism in Egypt*, Arabic translation by Abbas Mahmoud (Cairo, 1935), pp. 30-168.

15. Cf. Mustafa Abd Al-Raziq; see his article on 'Abduh in *Al Manar*, vol. XXIII, p. 524.

16. *Tarikh*, vol. II, pp. 7 and 46.

17. Ibid., p. 599.

18. *Tarikh*, vol. I, p. 12.

19. Ibid., p. 894.

20. The incident is reported in *Tarikh*, vol. I, pp. 896-7.

21. See, for instance, his article published after his return from Paris to Beirut in August 1885 concerning the Indian Question in which he echoes the political views of *Al 'Urwat al Wuthqa*. *Tarikh*, vol. II, pp. 374-9.

22. de Guerville, *La Nouvelle Egypte* (Paris, 1905), pp. 201-8. A part-translation appears in Osman Amin, *Ra'id al Fikr al Misri* (Cairo, 1955), pp. 251-3.

23. Rashid Ridha defends 'Abduh's position. See *Al Manar*, vol. XI, pp. 109 ff.

24. Cf. J. Schacht in the *Shorter Encyclopedia of Islam*, H.A.R. Gibb and J. H. Kramers (eds.), p. 407.

25. These ideas were widespread in the circle of Al-Afghani at the time. See, for instance, Abd Allah al-Nadim, *Sulafat al-Nadim* (Cairo, 1901), vol. I, pp. 99-120.

26. *Tarikh*, vol. II, p. 35.

27. Ibid., pp. 194-6.

28. *Tarikh*, vol. II, p. 199.

29. He quotes La Bruyère by name. Ibid., p. 194.

30. Blunt, *The Secret History*, p. 191.

31. As stated earlier, both legitimised rebellion. Further, neither advocated a Quraishi Khilafat. For the Kharijite view, see *Shorter Encyclopaedia of Islam*, p. 248, article by G. Levi della Vida.

32. *Tarikh*, vol. II, p. 221.

33. *Tarikh*, vol. I, p. 289.

34. Ibid., p. 219.

35. P. J. Vatikiotis, 'Muhammad 'Abduh and the Quest for a Muslim Humanism', *Arabica*, vol. IV, p. 58, points out that both Al-Afghani and 'Abduh subscribed to the ideas they published. He rightly rejects Goldziher's portrayal which in effect would make 'Abduh a mere secretary to Al-Afghani (E.I. 1st ed., vol. III, p. 678). Vatikiotis, however, falls into the same error by accepting 'Abduh's claim to have been against the political agitation and the advocacy of Pan-Islamism (while still writing in support of them).

36. Cf. P. J. Vatikiotis, op. cit., p. 59.

37. *Tarikh*, vol. II, pp. 288-9.

38. Ibid., pp. 335-6.

39. Ibid., pp. 237-49.

40. *Tarikh*, vol. II, p. 259 ff. and p. 377 ff.

41. Ibid., p. 227 ff. and p. 325 ff.

42. *Al Urwat al Wuthqa*, pp. 145-6. It is noticeable that the term *Ijma'* used here by Al-Afghani (and 'Abduh) differs from Al-Afghani's concept as related by Al Maghribi, op. cit., p. 60. Al-Bahay, op. cit., pp. 71-2, suggests that perhaps Al-Afghani in *Al Urwat* was acting more in the fashion of a popular leader than of a thinker.

43. See Ahmad Amin, *Yawm Al Islam* (Cairo, 1952), p. 112, also reports Gladstone as saying, 'The Qur'an must be eliminated.'

44. See, for instance, Ahmad Lutfi al-Sayyid, *Qessat Hayati* (Cairo, 1962), pp. 69-70, says, 'Europe need not fear this naive idea . . . it will not cause any worry to the European colonial power.' Also R. Ridha in *Al Manar*, vol. XIV, pp. 845-6.

45. *Tarikh*, vol. I, p. 34.

46. 'Abduh, *Al Islam Din Al-'Ilm Wa Al-Madaniyyah*, T. Tanahi (ed.) (Cairo, no date), p. 84. The book is roughly a new edition with some additions of *Al Islam Wa Al Nasraniyya Ma'a Al 'Ilm Wa Al-Madaniyyah* and *Al-Islam Wa Al-Radd Ala Muntagideeh*.

47. *Tarikh*, vol. I, p. 873, and Ali Merad, 'L'enseignement politique de Muhammad 'Abduh aux Algériens (1903)', *Orient*, no. 28. pp. 75-123, especially pp. 121-2.

48. The growth of the educational societies such as the Muhammidiyyah in Indonesia and the similar organisations in the Maghreb disguised their politics behind educational activities.

49. Abdal Rahman al Rafi'i, *Mustafa Kamil* (Cairo, 1939) reports Mustafa Kamil calling this policy the policy of double talk.

50. *Tarikh*, vol. I, p. 977.

51. Shaikh Muhammad Bakheet published two pamphlets in 1906 in which this occurs. See Ridha's review of them in *Al Manar*, vol. IX, p. 153.

52. *Tarikh*, vol. I, pp. 571-2.

53. As evidence for this view we note 'Abduh's criticism of Al-Afghani for his excessive honesty. *Tarikh*, vol. I, p. 896. He says that Al-Afghani should have attempted to satisfy Abu-al-Huda's cupidity and love for glory to blunt his opposition to reform. Surely he would have been prepared not to stand in Abbas's way had he not realised the futility of such a concession.

54. Al-Bahay, op. cit., p.150.

55. Cf. *Zu'ama al Islah*, pp. 311-15. Bernard Lewis, *The Middle East and the West* (London, 1963), p. 104, accepts Al-Bahay's position with regard to the cultural and intellectual influences where he also regards 'Abduh as opposing the Western onslaught in these fields.

56. Vol. V (1902), pp. 545-50.

57. Quoted by Ridha in *Al Manar*, vol. XI, p. 98.

58. *Al Islam Din Al-'Ilm Wa Al-Madaniyyah*, p. 100 and *Al Manar*, vol. V, p. 451.

59. *Al Islam*, p. 100-1, *Al Manar*, vol. V, loc cit.

60. *Al Islam*, p. 101 and *Al Manar*, vol. V, p. 452.

61. *Al Islam*, loc. cit.

62. Guido de Ruggiero, *The History of European Liberalism*, translated by R. G. Collingwood (Boston, 1961). Second printing, pp. 403-6.

63. *Tarikh*, vol. II, p. 200.

64. *Tarikh*, vol. II, p. L, Introduction.

65. *Tarikh*, vol. II, 1st ed., p. 9. 'Abduh says in the introduction to *Al Waridat* that the truth was clarified for him through 'the perfect sage and the personification of Truth our master Sayyid Jamal al-Din Al-Afghani'.

66. Orthodox commentators have since shown distaste for 'Abduh's liberal attitude towards the various sects. He was strongly criticised for his inclination towards philosophy and tolerance of heresy by Sulaiman Dunia in his *Al-Shaikh Muhammad 'Abduh bain al-falasifa wa'l Kalamiyyin* (2 vols., Cairo, 1958), which is an edition of 'Abduh's commentary. In the introduction, Dunia criticises 'Abduh's tolerance towards heresies. 'Abduh's own student and admirer Rashid Ridha criticised him for precisely the same position in vol. XXII, *Al Manar*, pp. 736-7. Dunia's views correspond very much with those of Rashid Ridha, and suggest that he might have been aware of Ridha's criticisms.

67. *Al-Manar*, loc. cit. Ridha says, 'He ['Abduh] was one of those deeply immersed in philosophy and mysticism but Allah guided him because of his sincerity to Salaf Mazhab.'

68. Although this writer sees little justification in the approach taken by Osman Amin in numerous works to the study of 'Abduh which lacks the developmental method, there is a sense of continuity in 'Abduh's thought. For instance, evidence of liberalism in his Sufi period may be noted in *Al Waridat's* introduction where he describes himself as having discarded the garb of the sects. *Tarikh*, vol. II, 1st ed., p. 9. And also in his support for free will in the same work where he disguises his views in this fashion, 'Allah is the doer where man is, and man is the doer where Allah is,' ibid., p. 25.

69. *Resalat Al-Tawhid*, p. 19. Osman Amin, *Ra'id Al Fikr Al-Misri* (Cairo, 1955), p. 62 ff. objects to this view and suggests that Rashid Ridha misrepresented 'Abduh's ideas which in turn led Max Horton to think little of 'Abduh as a philosopher. I find Amin's views more rhetorical than constructive. He states that Muhammad 'Abduh wanted to separate 'theology on the one hand from the commonly known philosophy on the other, or if you wish the imperfect knowledge of both philosophy and religion'!

70. *Resalat*, pp. 7-8.

71. It is not clear how many contributors to *Al Urwat* there were. G. Zaidan reports that Ibrahim Al Mwailhi contributed to it. *'Bunat al Nahdat al'Arabiyyah'*, a shortened version of his *Mashahir al-Sharq* (Cairo, no date), p. 175. Also it is reported that the Jewish Egyptian Nationalist, James Sanua, took a hand in it. See I. L. Gendzier, 'James Sanua, and Egyptian Nationalism', *M.E.J.*, vol. XV, no. 1, p. 27. Al-Afghani did contribute to Sanua's own paper *Abu Naddara* in Paris. See *Al Manar*, vol. XXVI, pp. 44-5.

72. *Tarikh*, vol. II, p. 235.

73. Summarised from *Al Islam Din Al 'Ilm wa Madaniyyah*, pp. 51-66.

74. Osman Amin, 'Muhammad 'Abduh's Apologetic for the Muslim Faith', *Minbar Al-Islam*, vol. II, no. 1, p. 19.

75. *Resalat al Tawhid*, the 17th ed. (Cairo, 1935), p. 52.

76. Ibid., p. 15.

77. Ibid., p. 20.

78. Ibid., p. 19.

79. Ibid., p. 23.

80. *Tarikh*, vol. II, pp. 37-45.

81. See B. D. McDonald, 'Al Ghazali', *E. I. Short*, p. 112 and Moh. bin Cheneb, 'Ibn Taimiya', p. 162.

82. *Al Manar*, vol. XXIII, p. 139. In his obituary of Abdul Karim Salman, Rashid Ridha makes it clear that he was superior to his colleague 'Abduh as regards ability and that 'Abduh's contribution was the result of hard work rather than innate intelligence. This, from Rashid Ridha, must be taken very seriously.

83. Cf. Nadav Safran, *Egypt in Search of Political Community* (London, 1961) p. 68 ff.

84. As in the case of Al-Farabi with regard to the apocryphal theology of Aristotle.

85. Cf. *Al Manar*, vol. VII, p. 292. 'Abduh says, 'There are two books: one created which is the universe, and one revealed which is the Qur'an and only through reason are we guided by this book to understand that one.'

86. Cf. *Al Manar*, vol. XXXII, p. 758 and *Tafsir Al Manar*, vol. I, p. 252. Cautious 'Abduh puts these views as mere possibilities.

87. *Resalat al Tawhid*, pp. 166-80.

88. He dismisses the popular outlook on this matter as the view of those who 'think that karamats . . . have become a type of profession in which Walis compete.' Ibid., p. 205.

89. 'Abduh, *Tafsir Juz 'Amma* (Cairo, 3rd ed., 1922), p. 90 describes the work of prophets a 'a reminder to the forgetful as to what Allah has instilled in his own nature'.

90. *Resalat*, p. 129.

91. Ibid., loc. cit.

92. Ibid., p. 128.

93. *Resalat*, pp. 166-7.

94. Ibid., p. 167.

95. *Resalat*, p. 169.

96. See Surah 3, Verse 112, and in other Surahs.

97. Surah 63, Verse 63. 'This is the law of Allah as manifested in the fortunes of those before you and the law of Allah shall never alter.'

98. Surah 13, Verse 13. 'Allah does not change the conditions of people until they change themselves.'

99. *Resalat*, pp. 176-8.

100. Ibid., pp. 200-1.

101. Ibid., p. 202.

102. Loc. cit.

103. Loc. cit.

104. For a discussion of this problem see Ahmad Amin, *Dhuha Al Islam*, vol. III, p. 47 ff., also Goldziher, *La loi et le dogme*, Arabic trans., pp. 106-7.

105. *Resalat*, p. 66.

106. Cf. *Al Iji al-Mawaqif* (Istanbul, 1286 A.H.) pp. 529-35, also Al Shahrastani, *Nihayat al Iqdam*, A. Guillaume trans. (Oxford, 1934), pp. 370-96.

107. *Resalat*, p. 66.

108. Loc. cit.

109. Loc. cit.

110. Loc. cit.

111. Ibid., p. 69.

112. Ibid., pp. 71-2.

113. Ibid., p. 73.

114. R. Caspar, 'Un aspect de la pensée musulmane moderne: le renouveau du Mu'tazilism', *Mélanges de l'Institut Dominican d'Etudes Orientales du Caire*, vol. IV, pp. 141-201, examines the relation between 'Abduh and the Mu'tazilites and labels him a neo-Mu'tazilite.

115. *Tarikh*, vol. II, p. 37 ff.

116. *Tarikh*, vol. II, p. 40.

117. Ibid., loc. cit.

118. Ibid., p. 43.

119. *Tarikh*, vol. II, p. 44.

120. *Tarikh*, vol. I, p. 145.

121. *Al Manar*, vol. XXIII, pp. 232-3.

122. *Tarikh*, vol. II, pp. 166-7.

123. Ibid., p. 451.

124. *Tarikh*, vol. II, p. 77.

125. Ibid., p. 76.
126. Ibid., p. 80.
127. Ibid., p. 156.
128. Ibid., p. 130.
129. Ibid., p. 156; he wrote strongly against the publication of books on magic and traditional epics and advised those who wished to read to read history instead or translations of European novels! See also his articles on 'Errors of the Wise', pp. 119-32.
130. Ibid., p. 256.
131. Ibid., pp. 215-341, especially pp. 268-75.
132. Ibid., p. 5.
133. Ibid., pp. 352-3.
134. Ibid., p. 353.
135. Ibid., p. 507.
136. Ibid., p. 511.
137. Ibid., p. 512. This is meant to strengthen the in-group feeling by arousing a degree of antipathy towards the out-group.
138. Ibid., p 517.
139. Ibid., p. 536.
140. Ibid., p. 537.
141. Ibid., p. 537.
142. Ibid., p. 548.
143. Ibid., p. 539.
144. Ibid., loc. cit.
145. Ibid., p. 541.
146. *Tarikh*, vol. II, p. 542. Perhaps this letter was behind the choice of 'Abduh to sit on the Al Azhar Committee.
147. Ibid., p. 545.
148. Ibid., loc. cit.
149. Ibid., p. 551.
150. *Tarikh*, vol. I, p. 425.
151. *Tarikh*, vol. I, p. 426.
152. The booklet is published in toto in *Tarikh*, vol. I, pp. 430-92.
153. *Al Manar*, vol. VIII, pp. 234-7. These sentences occur in a letter from Rashid Ridha to Muhsin Al Mulk of India.
154. *Tarikh*, vol. I, p. 501.
155. For the views of Cromer on Islam, which were exceptionally antagonistic, see R. T. Tignor,'Lord Cromer on Islam', *The Muslim World*, vol. III, pp. 223-33.
156. *Tarikh*, vol. I, p. 1034.
157. Joseph Schacht, 'The Law' in *Unity and Variety in Muslim Civilization* G. E. von Grunebaum (ed) (Chicago, 1955), p. 82, says, 'The impact of European ideas in the Islamic world in the present century, however, has brought about effects of a vastly different, unprecedented and irrevocable kind.'
158. *Zu'ama al Islah*, p. 114.
159. Muhammad 'Ali weakened the political as well as the social position of the *ulema* by dividing them and depriving them of their leader, 'Umar Makram. See A. Al-Rafi'i, *'Asr Muhammad 'Ali* (Cairo, 1930), pp. 71-95. Compare his position with that of Selim III and Mahmoud II of Turkey. See U. Heyd, 'The Ottoman Ulemas and Westernization' in *Studies in Islamic History and Civilization* (Jerusalem, 1961) U. Heyd (ed.), p. 69 ff. The co-operation of the *ulema* in Turkey was important for the introduction of reform.
160. M. Al-Bahay, op. cit., pp. 71-2.
161. The essence of the school's attack on Taqlid is an attack on an established Ijma'. See I. Goldziher's comments on the Wahabbis in *La Loi et Le Dogme*

en Islam, trans. by Muhammad Yusuf Musa *et. al.* (Cairo, 2nd ed., 1959), p. 269 Also the view of Rashid Ridha concerning Ijma'. See his *Yusr al Islam* (Cairo, 1928), p. 3.

162. *Tarikh*, vol. I, p. 689. The Transvaal Fatwa was given in reply to a question sent to 'Abduh by an Indian living in that country asking as to whether an animal slaughtered by a Christian would be *Halal* for a Muslim to eat. 'Abduh answered in the affirmative. His enemies accused him of deviating from Muslim law. Ridha comments on the Transvaal Fatwa saying that 'It is supported by the Qur'an, the Sunna and the practice of the Salaf and Khalaf and their words.' Charles Adams, op. cit., p. 76 (Arabic translation) described his fatwas as representing a spirit of independence. This must be qualified by the statement above.

163. *Tarikh*, vol. I, p. 647.

164. Ibid., p. 710 ff.

165. Ibid., p. 716, and 'Abdul Hafiz al Fasi, *Riyad al-Janna aw al mudhish al mutrib* (Fez, 1350 A.H.) pp. 48-50.

166. Ibid., p. 939.

167. *Al Manar,* vol. VIII, p. 416 and Adams, op. cit., pp. 64-5.

168. *Al Islam*, p. 138.

169. Ibid., p. 138.

170. *Tarikh*, vol. I, p. 940.

171. Ibid., p. 940.

172. Ibid., p. 941.

173. Ibid., p. 560.

174. Ibid., p. 612, fn. 1.

175. Ibid., p. 557.

176. *Tarikh*, vol. II, p. 163.

177. Ibid., p. 469.

178. *Tarikh*, vol. I, p. 614.

179. *Resalat,* pp. 72-3.

180. Cf. Osman Amin, op. cit., pp. 115-16.

181. See, for instance, Osman Amin, *Muhammad 'Abduh* (Cairo, 1945). Also by the same author, *Ra'is al Fikr al Misri* (Cairo, 1955) and numerous other articles by him. Also Muhammad Al Bahay, *Muhammad 'Abduh, Erziehungsmethode zum national-bewusstsein* (Hamburg, 1936) and his *Modern Muslim Thought*. See also J. Schacht, 'Muhammad 'Abduh', in the *Encyclopaedia of Islam*. Also Charles Adams, *Islam and Modernism in Modern Egypt,* pp. 20-168 (Arabic trans.).

182. See for instance quotations by Martin Lings in *A Moslem Saint of the Twentieth Century* (London, 1961), p. 110, where 'Abduh is quoted as saying that 'The Sufis are concerned with the cure of hearts and purification from all that obstructs the inward eye.' And also 'I do not deny, my brother, the existence of many intruders among the Sufis – only too many – who deserve censure, and if you had concentrated on these, no one could have blamed you.'

183. *Tarikh*, vol. I, pp. 928-9, also *Tafsir,* vol. II, p. 165.

184. *Tarikh,* vol. I, p. 928. H.A.R. Gibb utilises this view on his 'An Interpretation of Islamic History', *The Muslim World*, vol. XLV, pp. 129-33.

185. Ibid., p. 929.

186. See the comment on him by the distinguished conservative Al-Dijwi in *Al Manar*, vol. XXXIII, p. 678, quoted from *Nur Al Islam*. There he regrets 'Abduh's tendency to imitate every European idea before it was proved by conclusive evidence.

187. His *Waridat*, however, had a positive contribution in influencing Shaikh Ahmad Al-'Alawi. See M. Lings, op. cit., p. 132, fn. 1.

188. His theoretical adoption of the Maliki principle basing legislation concerning mundane matters on utility could not be upheld completely. My contention as to his limited influence is contradicted by several who attribute every development on the law of the Arab or Muslim world to 'Abduh. See, for instance, N. J. Coulson, 'A History of Islamic Law', *Islamic Surveys*, no. 2 (Edinburgh 1964), pp. 210-11, where the writer suggests that reforms in Tunisian and Syrian personal law were based on the views of 'Abduh.

189. See Ahmad, *The Intellectual Origins of Egyptian Nationalism*, p. 91, where he says *Al-Jaridah* was never a popular paper.

190. *Al Manar*, vol. X, p. 15.

191. *Al Manar*, vol. XXVIII, p. 588 ff. Charles Adams, op. cit., pp. 218-21 (Arabic. trans.). Also Osman Amin, *'Ra'id'*, pp. 209-11.

192. Cf. Ahmad Amin, *Zu'ama*, p. 108.

193. Shaikh Mustafa Al-Maraghi, Rector of Al Azhar 1928-29 and 1935-45. The reforms introduced under the rectorship of another student of 'Abduh, Shaikh Al-Zawahari, 1930-5, were inspired more by the example of the University than by 'Abduh. Osman Amin, *Ra'id*, pp. 212-14 cites Zawahiri as the representative of what he called 'Abduh's religious school. Rashid Ridha would have objected to this as Zawahiri was accused of equivocation in support of 'Abduh. See *Al Manar*, vol. VIII, p. 114 and 'Al Manar Wa Al-Azhar' (Cairo, 1935) records a quarrel between Ridha and Al Azhar under Shaikh Zawahiri.

194. Cf. H.A.R. Gibb, *Studies on the Civilization of Islam* (London, 1962), p. 225, Section 13, *Studies in Contemporary Arabic Literature*.

195. See, for instance, his support for monogamy in *Tafsir*, vol. IV, pp. 348-9.

196. See *Al Manar*, vol. XXXI, p. 352, also Lufti Al-Sayyid, *Qessat Hayati* (Cairo, 1962), p. 37. Ridha says that 'Abduh saw this book before its publication and corrected the Arabic, but not his second book. Could this account also for the difference between the two books? Rashid Ridha was noticeably unenthusiastic about the view of Qassim Amin and he apologised for him by suggesting that he wanted less than he advocated, but demanded more to stimulate his readers who were at the extreme end of conservatism to move into a position of moderation. Had Qassim Amin belonged to a different group, Ridha would not have been so mild. *Al Manar*, vol. IV, pp. 31-2.

197. See Rashid Ridha below.

198. Cf. A. Hourani, op. cit., p. 168. The two books appeared in 1899 and 1901 respectively.

199. Osman Amin, for instance, in *Ra'id*, p. 222, accuses Ridha of deviating from the path of 'Abduh with regard to Ridha's opposition to Taha Husain and 'Ali Abd Al-Raziq.

200. Cf. H. Laoust, *Essai sur les doctrines sociales et politiques d'Ibn Taimiya* (Cairo, 1939), p. 562.

201. *Tarikh*, vol. II, pp. 388-9.

202. *Tarikh*, vol. I, p. 890. 'Abduh is said to have been careful about voicing his opinions and did not write or say all that he believed.

203. See I. Abu-Lughod, *Arab Rediscovery of Europe* (Princeton, 1963), p. 21.

204. A. M. Broadly, *How We Defended 'Urabi and His Friends* (London, 1884), p. 227, reports 'Urabi as saying that 'Abduh's head was more fit for a hat than a turban. Added to this is the bad relationship between 'Abduh and the spokesman of the revolutionary followers of Al-Afghani, Adib Ishaq. See 'Documents Inédits', frame no. 63. Also *Tarikh*, vol. II, p. 601. The names were omitted by Rashid Ridha.

205. Cf. M. Al Khafif, op. cit., p. 555. At a meeting between 'Urabi and 'Abduh, arranged by Blunt, 'Urabi accused 'Abduh of writing with the purpose of

pleasing the Khedive.

206. *Modern Egypt*, vol. II, p. 179.

207. To name a few, Abd Allah Al-Nadim, a brilliant speaker and journalist and the orator of the Rebellion, and Adib Ishaq the gifted writer and journalist and the official spokesman of the Constitutionalists. Both in their ways were much more respected than 'Abduh.

208. *Tarikh*, vol. II, p. 69 ff., especially p. 71.

209. Charles Adams, op. cit., p. 11 (Arabic trans.).

210. See, for instance, M. Al Bahay, op. cit., p. 150.

211. For discussion of the *Tafsir*, see I. Golziher, *Richtungen der Islamischen Koranauslegung* (Leiden, 1920), Arabic trans. *Al Najjar*, pp. 348 ff. Also J.M.S. Baljon, *Modern Muslim Koran Interpretation (1880-1960)* (Leiden, 1961), *passim*, and A. M. Shehatah, *Manhaj Al Imam Muhammad 'Abduh fī Tafsir Al Qur'an Al Karim* (Cairo, 1963), and J. Jomier,*Le Commentaire Coranique du Manar* (Paris, 1954).

212. Osman Amin, op. cit., p. 55, fn. 2, describes this tendency as *pragmatic humanism* and equates 'Abduh with the leaders of pragmatism such as William James and F.K.S. Schiller. This trend, however, was inspired by Ibn Taimiya rather than by an acquaintance with modern thought.

213. *Tarikh*, vol. I, pp. 587-8. Ridha states that he had selected 'Abduh for the leadership of the *Umma* and was determined to build him up for that position.

214. On the activities of the Muhammadiyyah see *Indonesiche Documentatie*, vol. III, no. XIX, p. 720 (The Hague, 1952). The report gives the numerical strength of the movement as 159,000 and 2,000 schools under its control.

215. *Tarikh*, vol. I, p. 11.

216. As for instance the questions on the attributes of God. See *Resalat*, p. 52, where he dismisses the question of whether the attribute should be regarded as separate or identical with the Godhead as being beyond human reason.

217. Cf. Osman Amin, *Ra'id*, p. 61-2.

218. When Shanqiti objected to 'Abduh's Mu'tazilite views in regarding the Qur'an as being created not eternal, 'Abduh had it removed in the second and subsequent editions of the *Resalat*. See *Tarikh*, vol. I, p. 963.

219. As for instance his evolutionist interpretation of prophecy and religion. He utilises evolutionist theory in many places of the *Tafsir*. See Adams, op. cit., p. 130 ff.

220. 'Abduh was suspected by Cromer, *Modern Egypt*, vol. II, p. 181, as being agnostic. His friend, W. S. Blunt, quoted by Thomas J. Assad in *3 Victorian Travellers* (London, 1964), pp. 98-9, saw him as having no faith in Islam. Many of his contemporary *ulema* have also doubted his faith. See also Margoliouth's review of Adams' *Islam and Modernism* in the *International Review of Missions*, vol. XXII, pp. 421-2.

221. Op. cit., p. 161 ff., especially p. 163.

222. *Al Islam*, p. 148.

223. *Ra'id*, p. 61.

224. Op. cit., p. 163.

225. The dispute between Manfaluti and Qassim Amin reported by H.A.R. Gibb, op. cit., p. 265, is an example of this. It reflects an attitude to social policy on the part of some of 'Abduh's friends lacking in dynamism which is concomitant with the scientific attitude.

226. Cf. N. Safran, op. cit., p. 69.

227. See Charles Adams, op. cit., pp. 238-9.

228. *Tafsir Al Manar*, vol. IV, p. 350.

229. Bashir Ahmad Dar, op. cit., p. 272 ff.

152 Notes

230. *Tarikh*, vol. I, Introduction p. nun. Blunt holds a similar view as shown by his remark to Harold Spender of the *Daily Chronicle* that "Abduh was like Cardinal Manning, trading religion for politics. He was so clever that he forced the Khedive and Lord Cromer to appoint him head of the *ulema* in Egypt.' *Tarikh*, vol. III, p. 181.

CHAPTER 3

1. *Tarikh*, vol. I, p. 1013, states that 'Abduh found followings to himself in Tunisia and Algeria who knew him only through *Al Manar*.
2. *Al Manar*, XXVIII, p. 65, also Adams, op. cit., p. 169.
3. Adams, op. cit., pp. 169-70.
4. *Al Manar*, vol. XXXIII, p. 354.
5. Ibid., pp. 357-72. No doubt he was prompted into publishing these aspects, previously unknown in his life, as a sort of self-defence against accusations by the traditionalists of heresy.
6. Op. cit., p. 354.
7. *Tarikh*, vol. I, p. 85, and Adams, op. cit., p. 171.
8. *Tarikh*, vol. I, p. 84.
9. Ibid., pp. 85-7, contains the letter and commentary. The quotation is from p. 82.
10. Ibid., pp. 996-7.
11. Ibid., p. 1000.
12. Ibid., p. 1001.
13. Ibid., p. 1022.
14. *Al Manar*, vol. I, 2nd ed., p. 4, and Adams, op. cit., p. 172.
15. *Al Manar*, vol. I, 2nd ed., pp. 11 and 12.
16. Goldziher as quoted by Adams, op. cit., p. 173.
17. *Tarikh*, vol. I, p. 514.
18. Perhaps 'Abduh was himself responsible for this delusion by invariably approving what Ridha wrote in his name. Ibid., p. 1018.
19. See, for instance, *Al Manar*, vol. XXVII, p. 622, where he quoted an unnamed Jew stating that the University represented anti-religious trends. Similar views are also held by a more recent writer, namely Dr Al Bahay, op. cit., p. 101.
20. *Al Manar*, vol. VIII, p. 478. Also Adams, op. cit., p. 176.
21. *Al Manar*, vol. VIII, p. 478.
22. *Al Manar*, vol. XXXII, p. 317.
23. *Al Manar*, vol. XXXIII, p. 534. Rashid Ridha mentions that Maraghi asked him to write a report on the advisability of an Azhar magazine, which he did. He was not, however, invited to hold any official post.
24. See Ridha, *Al Manar wa Al- Azhar* (Cairo, 1353 A.H.), serialised in *Al Manar*, vols. XXXI and XXXII.
25. *Tarikh*, vol. I, pp. 620-1 related the story that Isma'il requested Rifa'a Al-Tahtawi to persuade the *ulema* to codify the Shari'a law but he refused. (Isma'il in reality did not need any such codification as Muslim law had already been codified in the famous Majalah and was being applied in Ottoman domains.)
26. Cf. J.N.D. Anderson, 'The Shari'a and Civil Law', *The Islamic Quarterly*, vol. I, p. 29.
27. *Al Manar*, vol. XII, p. 239.
28. *Al Manar*, vol. XIV p. 343.
29. Rashid Ridha, the introduction to *Al Mughni* by Al Muwaffaq (Cairo, 1925), p. 15.
30. *Al Mughni*, p. 16.

31. *Al Manar*, vol. XIV, p. 344.

32. *Al Mughni*, p. 18.

33. *Al Manar*, vol. IV, p. 210.

34. Loc. cit.

35. *Al Manar*, vol. IX, p. 745. The treatise proper runs to p. 770.

36. Loc. cit.

37. *Al Manar*, vol. XXX, p. 704 ff. Ridha argues against M. Azmi who claimed that some of the *ulema* considered that Maslaha superseded even unambiguous texts. Ridha rejects both the contents of the claim and that any of the *ulema* supported it. As we know, Al Tawfi put Maslaha above the texts. (See Mustafa Zaid, *Al Maslaha Fi Al Tashri' Al Islami* (Cairo, 1954), pp. 63-4.) Early in the century (1909) Ridha approvingly published Al Tawfi's treatise and appeared to support the same view in his 'Muhawarat al Muslih Wa Al Muqallid', *Al Manar*, vol. IV. This was in the heyday of liberalism. His position appears to have changed somewhat in the twenties and thirties where the emphasis on the authority of the texts and the restriction on Maslaha as an independent operative concept has become marked. This may be a reaction to the excesses of the modernists and Westernisers. This line of analysis, however, will not be pursued further since Ridha failed to reflect these two phases in his rulings on specific issues.

38. Ridha, *Yusr Al Islam* (Cairo, 1928), Introduction, pp. b, g and h.

39. Ibid., Introduction pp. z, a, y and e.

40. Ibid., p. 3.

41. Loc. cit.

42. Loc. cit.

43. Loc. cit.

44. *Al Manar*, vol. XXIX, p. 424.

45. His book, *Muhawarat al Muslih Wa Al Muqallid*, relies heavily on Ibn Al-Qayyim, the Hanbali scholar, as he himself admits in the introduction (*Al Manar*, vol. IX, p. 823), whereas his *Yusr Al Islam* is a collection of opinions largely drawn from the same school.

46. *Yusr Al Islam*, pp. 17-18.

47. Ibid., p. 79.

48. Ibid., loc. cit. Rashid Ridha gives the authority to Ulu Al Amr in wordly affairs. Obedience to them is conditioned by them not contradicting the law.

49. Ibid., pp. 78-9.

50. Ibid., pp. 37-75. He quotes approvingly from Ibn Al Qayyim.

51. *Al Manar*, vol. XIV, p. 23.

52. *Al Manar*, vol. X, p. 287 ff. and vol. XXIII, p. 187 ff. and in various places in *Tafsir Al Manar*. See Jomier, 'Le commentaire', p. 290.

53. *Al Manar*, vol. XXVII, p. 346, also Vol. VII, pp. 384-8 and vol. VIII, p. 588.

54. *Al Manar*, vol. VII, p. 28.

55. *Yusr Al Islam*, pp. 72-3.

56. *Nida' Ila Al-jins Al-Latif* (Cairo, 1351 A.H.), p. 121.

57. *Al Manar*, vol. XXX, p. 610 fn.

58. *Al Wahy Al Muhamadi*, 3rd ed., p. 283.

59. *Al Manar*, vol. XXX, p. 780.

60. M. Kerr, 'Rashid Ridha and Legal Reforms', *The Muslim World*, vol. I, p. 180.

61. *Al Manar*, vol. XXIV, p. 111.

62. *Al Manar*, vols. XXXI and XXXII carry the arguments between Ridha and Al Dijwi. The articles were later published in the separate book *Al Manar Wa Al-Azhar*.

63. The effort of Al Ghazali in reconciling Sufism and orthodoxy may be

cited as an example. See H.A.R. Gibb, 'An Interpretation of Islamic History',
The Muslim World, vol. XIV, pp. 129-30.

64. See, for instance, *Al Manar*, vol. VIII, p. 620, where he says, 'The people
have no longer any need for most of the theories contained in Ash'arite books.'

65. *Al Wahy Al Muhamadi*, 3rd ed., p. 360.

66. Ibid., pp. 8 and 9.

67. Ibid., p. 10.

68. Ibid., p. 17 ff.

69. Ibid., pp. 19 and 20.

70. Ibid., p. 62. The Qur'an is, however, exempt from this generalisation as
it does not as a miraculous book tax the scientific mind in the same way as, say,
the miracle of the break-up of the moon.

71. Ibid., p. 255 ff.

72. Ibid., p. 289 ff.

73. *Al Manar*, vol. XXIII, p. 189.

74. On Al Ghazali see *Al Manar*, vol. V, pp. 762-8 and on the Ash'ari see
vol. IX, pp. 109-10. There Rashid Ridha attributes this view to the later followers
of Ash'ari and not to him. Under the influence of nineteenth-century rationalism,
Muslim reformists and modernists accepted the principle of causality without
looking deeper into its implications. (The probable exception is Ahmad Khan.)
'Abduh and Rashid Ridha did not appreciate fully the difficulty of the Ash'arites.
For discussion of the problem of causality in Muslim thought see Majid Fakhry,
Islamic Occasionalism (London, 1958), pp. 56 ff. *et passim.*

75. *Al Manar*, vol. VIII, p. 620.

76. *Al-Wahy*, p. 199. The idea put forward previously by Dr M. T. Sidqi in
Al Manar, vol. XII, p. 120.

77. Ibid., p. 62.

78. Ibid., p. 201.

79. *Al Manar*, vol. I, p. 274 and Adams, op. cit., p. 186.

80. *Al Manar*, vol. XIV, pp. 809-10.

81. Ibid., p. 810.

82. Ibid., p. 809.

83. Ibid., p. 813.

84. Ibid.,pp. 812-16.

85. Ibid., p. 811.

86. Ibid., pp. 786 and 801, and Adams, op. cit., p. 188. These ideas were not
without influence on the reform of Al Azhar.

87. *Al Manar*, vol. XXXV. The obituary of Rashid Ridha by his cousin Sayyid
Abd Al-Rahman 'Asin, p. 486.

88. *Al Manar*, vol. XXX, p. 115 ff.

89. Guido de Ruggiero, op. cit., p. 93 ff. and p. 158 ff.

90. *Tarikh*, vol. I, p. 915. Ridha says that he and 'Abduh aimed at Arab
independence but without foreign interference or enmity with the Turks.

91. The suspicions surrounding Rashid Ridha reached far and wide. See, for
instance, the recently uncovered letter from Abu Al Kalam Azad to Ridha accusing him of supporting the decentralisation party and thus betraying his previously
announced support for the Caliphate. A. Al-Nimr, 'Mawlana Azad Wal Khilafa',
Majallat Al Azhar, vol. XXXV, Oct. 1963, p. 307.

92. See, for instance, the arguments between Rashid Ridha and the Nationalist
Party, notably A. Jawish, concerning the 'Madrassat Al Da'wah', *Al Manar*, vol.
XIV, pp. 40 and 121 ff.

93. See his comments, *Al Manar*, vol. XXIII, p. 695.

94. See, for instance, *Al Manar*, vol. XXXIII, pp. 317-18 where he suggests
an elaborate Sayyid university to train specialists in all the sciences and arts,

'religious and worldly and the skills upon which civilization is based in this age'. He ends thus: 'Only then will the *Umma* know that the Sayyids are her masters and leaders.' He puts a similar suggestion in his writing on 'Al Khilafat', where he advises the creation of a *mujtahid* school to prepare Quraishis to hold the office of Caliph. *Al Manar*, vol. XXIV, pp. 110-11.

95. He took part in the 'Decentralization Party' and may have participated in conspiracies against the Ottomans. After the war he played a prominent part in Syrian politics which he records in *Al Manar*, vols. XXII and XXIII, under the title 'The Syrian Journey', and also 'The European Journey'. Abd Al-Muta'l Al-Saidi in his *Al Mujaddidun Fi'l Islam Min'al Qarn Al Awwal Ila'l Rabi Ashar* (Cairo, no date), pp. 542-3, reports Rashid Ridha as supporting King Fuad's claim to the Caliphate. This would have implemented the ideas of W.S. Blunt who aimed at creating an Arab Caliphate under the aegis of the British. Since Blunt's ideas expounded in his *The Future of Islam* (London, 1882), were derived from 'Abduh's (see A. Hourani, op. cit., p. 155) it is conceivable that Al Sa'idi's report is correct. This need not reflect on Ridha. In the desperate situation after the fall of the Caliphate, Ridha might have felt that its continuation, even on such a basis, was better than its complete disappearance. The relationship between Sharif Hussain and Ridha is also a source of confusion. There is no doubt that Ridha supported Hussain's original moves until it became evident that the British had defaulted in their promises.

96. (Cairo, 1341 A.H.). Translated into French by H. Laoust under the title *Le califat dans la doctrine de Rashid Ridha* (Beirut, 1938). References are made to the *Al Manar* serialisation.

97. *Al Manar*, vol. XXIII, p. 729.

98. Ibid., loc. cit.

99. Ibid., pp. 730-52.

100. *Al Manar*, vol. XXIV, p. 352.

101. Ibid., p. 353.

102. Ibid., loc. cit.

103. Ibid., p. 353.

104. *Al Manar*, vol. XXIV, p. 354. Ridha reports the encounter between 'Abduh Al-Dawlah the Turk and the Abbasid Caliph Al-Ta'i'. The Turk, while showing all veneration and respect, divested the Caliph of all his authority. This Rashid Ridha appears to suggest was done voluntarily by the Caliph. Had the Caliph had a better moral fibre, Rashid Ridha appears to imply, then he would have retained the powers of his office.

105. Ibid., p. 355.

106. Ibid., loc. cit.

107. Ibid., p. 646.

108. Ibid., pp. 460-1.

109. Ibid., p. 353.

110. Ibid., p. 373.

111. Ibid., p. 198.

112. *Al Manar*, vol. XXIII, p. 731, where he quotes the Tradition, 'whoever dies not having given Bay'a dies a Jahiliyya death.'

113. *Al Manar*, vol. XIV, p. 9.

114. Ibid., p. 13.

115. *Tafsir.*, vol. V. p. 190.

116. Ibid., pp. 190-1. These views are attributed to 'Abduh. Rashid Ridha also subscribed to them.

117. *Al Manar*, vol. XIV, pp. 59-60.

118. *Al Manar*, vol. XXIV, p. 59.

119. *Tafsir*, vol. V, p. 190.

120. *Al Manar*, vol. XXIV, pp. 61-2.

121. Ibid., p. 48 ff.

122. *Al Manar*, vol. XXIII, pp. 738-44.

123. *Al Manar*, vol. XXIV, p. 110.

124. Ibid., p. 119.

125. Cf. Malcolm Kerr, 'Arab Radical Notions of Democracy' in *Middle Eastern Affairs No. 3, St Antony's Papers no. 16*, p. 15.

126. *Tafsir*, vol. V, p. 200 and *Al Manar*, vol. XIV, p. 14.

127. *Tafsir*, vol. V, p. 199. These views are 'Abduh's but Ridha subscribes to them also.

128. Emile Tyan, *Institutions du droit public musulman*, vol. II: *Sultanat et califat* (Paris, 1956), p. 264, fn. 2.

129. Louis Gardet, *La cité musulmane: vie sociale et politique* (Paris, 1954), p. 352.

130. For an evaluation of Al Mawardi's theory see Gibb, *Studies on the Civilization of Islam* (London, 1962), pp. 151-64, especially pp. 162-3.

131. *Al Manar*, vol. XXIV, pp. 259-61.

132. *Al Manar*, vol. XII, pp. 608-9.

133. *Al Manar*, vol. XXIV, p. 62.

134. *Al Manar,* vol. XIV, pp. 197-200.

135. Ibid., p. 199.

136. During this period the conflict between Egypt and Britain was manifested in a triangular power struggle: the British, the Palace and the Wafd.

137. See G. Kampffmeyer in H.A.R. Gibb, *Whither Islam?*, Ch. 3 (London, 1932). Also *Al Manar*, vol. XXVIII, p. 788 ff. Ridha says he thought of inaugurating one during the war but the military authorities refused permission.

138. *Al-Manar*, vol. XXVI, pp. 100-4.

139. N. Safran, op. cit., pp. 165-80.

140. S. Arslan says, 'Although he [Ridha] may not be the equal of 'Abduh and Afghani in the logical sciences ('Ulum 'Aqliyyah), he outstripped them both in the volume of writing.' *Rashid Ridha Aw Ikha Arba'ina Sanatan* (Damascus, 1937), p. 255.

141. Cf. *Tafsir,* vol. I, p. 284.

142. See reference to this in *Al Manar*, vol. XXXIII, pp. 529-30.

143. See, for instance, his bitter dispute with the Shi'is. *Al Manar*, vol. IX, pp. 424 ff.

144. *Al Manar*, vol. IX, p. 20.

145. Cf. R. A. Hourani, Introduction to J. M. Ahmed, op. cit., p. X.

146. Al-Afghani versus Renan, 'Abduh versus Hanotaux and Renan, Rashid Ridha versus Dermingham, even Al-Afghani's *Al Radd*, etc. may be regarded as a discussion of European ideas.

147. *Tarikh.*, vol. I, p. 799.

INDEX

The entries for the three main characters are quasi-biographical, matters mainly concerned with the individual being placed there: the reader should seek his reference in the main index first, but turn to the three principal names' entries if the subject required refers to the man concerned.

DATE DUE